American
CAR HAULERS

THE CRESTLINE SERIES

American CAR HAULERS

Richard J. Copello

MBI Publishing Company

First published in 2000 by MBI Publishing Company, 729 Prospect Avenue, PO Box 1, Osceola, WI 54020-0001 USA

MBI Publishing Company books are also available at discounts in bulk quantity for industrial or sales-promotional use. For details write to Special Sales Manager at Motorbooks International Wholesalers & Distributors, 729 Prospect Avenue, PO Box 1, Osceola, WI 54020-0001 USA.

Library of Congress Cataloging-in-Publication Data
    Copello, Richard J.
        American car haulers / Richard J. Copello
        p. cm. — (The crestline series)
        Includes index.
        ISBN 0-7603-0694-X (paperback : alk. paper)
            1. Tractor trailer combinations—United States—
    History. I. Title. II. Series.

        TL230.5.T73   C67   2000
        629.224'0973—dc21   99-054249

On the front cover: Loaded with new 1955 Mercurys, this Convoy Company six-car rig is ready to move out. The tractor is a 1955 Ford F-800 "Big Job" V-8 with Custom Cab equipment and a sleeper box. Note the typical 1955 colors on the Mercurys. *Ackroyd Photography Inc.*

On the back cover: A Montpelier Dodge owned by Automobile Shippers Inc. of Detroit carrying 1938 Plymouths. A Ford tilt cab pulling a trailer full of 1959 Lincolns and Mercury station wagons. *Neil Sherff* A 1957 Ford F-800 "Big Job" transporting 1960 Ford Falcons. *Ackroyd Photography Inc.* A WHITEGMC WG tractor with a trailer full of 1992 Corvettes.

Printed in China

Contents

Acknowledgments

This book could not have been possible had it not been for the help of several hundred individuals with whom I've corresponded in the past 15 years. Although many of the photos in this book came from a core group of about 20 people, many more in my collection came from the friends I know only through the mail. I will try to acknowledge as many as possible.

Ted Ahrens is the car hauler enthusiast extraordinary. Almost everything in this book related to W. R. Arthur or Janesville Auto Transport Company came by way of Ted. He has gone so far as to buy and single-handedly restore a 1953 Stuart four-car trailer in Arthur's colors. In addition, he has the 1955 Chevrolet (first series) tractor to pull it and four period Chevrolets to fill it. I must also thank Ted for the encouragement to do this book.

For many years, Phillip Baumgarten was the only person I knew, other than myself, who had an interest in auto carriers. He was involved in several transport firms immediately before and after World War II. The information that he has provided has been invaluable. However, more valuable are his personal recollections of events in the 1940s and 1950s. Phil has also encouraged me, and I thank him for everything.

With the exception of a few photographs borrowed from Ron Adams and Donald Wood, most of the photos in this book came from my collection of photos, which number in the thousands. If they were marked as to their origin, or if I remembered when they came from, I've given credit in the caption. If I've missed anyone or gave credit incorrectly, please contact me and I'll correct the error in future editions.

Four individuals' names, Ron Adams, Harry Patterson, Neil Sherff, and Joe Wanchura appear quite often in the credit lines. Long before I snapped my first auto carrier photo, these guys were out photographing every truck they could. Fortunately, among the many thousands of rigs they shot, they got a few auto transporters. The color shots from Neil and Joe in the 1950s are priceless. Ron and Harry have helped cover the carrier activity of the 1960s and later. Without their help, the early chapters could not have been illustrated. Thank you, guys.

The following people, most of whom are members of the American Truck Historical Society, have supplied photos or information directly related to this publication: Bob Baciulis, Owen Barcomb, Bruce Brunner, Don Bunn, Mark Campbell, Robert Farrell of the National Auto Transporters Association, Dave Faust, Michael Haeder, John Heistand, Elliott Kahn, Rick Manz, Russ MacNeil, Paul McLaughlin, Gary Morton, Allen Neamtz, Freddie Nelson, Jim Rowe (JR), Glenn Shaffer, Francois Spenard, Mark Waterman, Mark Wayman, and Fred Yokel. A sincere thank you to everyone.

—*Richard J. Copello*

Introduction

Most of us, at one time or another, have looked at a loaded car carrier and admired the new autos in transit. This book is about those car carriers and the vehicles they haul. It covers their development from the early days of hard rubber tires and open cabs to today's rigs with low-profile rubber and air-conditioned cabs.

Since this book is based mainly on photos, I've tried to show a variety of vehicles in transit from each time period. Look closely at the photos, maybe you'll see an auto you once owned on board one of these rigs. At least, maybe one similar. That's what I wanted this book to be about—memories.

CHAPTER 1

Before 1930

The Early Days

As the end of the nineteenth century grew near, automotive pioneers were perfecting the first gasoline-powered automobiles. Basically motorized buggies, they were often referred to as "horseless carriages." The first motor trucks appeared about 1900, but their usefulness was limited by the lack of good roads. In fact, hard-surfaced roads usually ended at the city limits, and travel into rural areas was possible only in dry weather. It would be many years until intercity trucking was possible on a large scale.

In 1908, Henry Ford began production of his Model T, America's first affordable mass-produced automobile. By 1913, Ford's assembly plant was turning out 1,000 Model Ts each workday. These early motor vehicles were usually delivered to dealers by rail or driveaway.

After the mid-1800s, America's railroad system had built a vast network of tracks crossing the nation. For interstate shipments, rail was the primary form of transporting nearly every commodity, including autos. Although some early autos were shipped on open railroad flatcars, a variation of the standard boxcar was devveloped for automobile transportation. These units offered better protection from the elements and could also be used to transport general freight. These boxcars could transport two, three, or four autos. When three or four autos were transported, the first two were backed into opposite ends of the boxcar and their front ends were raised using a block and tackle. This created space for one or two more autos to be placed in the center of the car. Everything had to be blocked in place and tied down to prevent damage in transit. Most auto manufacturers shipped their autos F.O.B. the assembly plant, meaning that the rail transport was at the dealer's expense. Upon arrival at their destination, he also had the

An early attempt at truckaway. Note the loading skids, which appear to be 2X6 lumber, straining under the auto's weight.
The truck is a 1919 White chain-drive. *Volvo-White*

Transportation Contractors, Inc., delivered unassembled Model T Fords on this 1922 Sterling. The dealer would perform the final assembly. This company later became University Overland Express, a major New England carrier of Ford products. *Nu Car Carriers*

A four-car load on an early Model A Ford and trailer. Note the open cab and extra axle on the tractor. Also note the trailer's overhang. The driver had to use extreme care when turning in congested areas, as the overhang would swing in the opposite direction to the turn.

responsibility for locating and unloading the rail car. Unloading was a difficult and a time-consuming operation that most dealers did not want to deal with. For that reason, companies that offered to perform this service on the dealer's behalf began to spring up. In the Chicago area, one of the earliest such companies was Arthur and Black. W. R. Arthur had been employed in the traffic department of the Elgin Motor Car Company in Elgin, Illinois. That company ceased operations in 1921 and Arthur found himself out of work. Relying on his traffic department experience, he, his wife Hazel, and a Mr. Black established an unloading and delivery company serving the Chicago area.

The autos that didn't go by rail were usually driven to their destination, a method of delivery called "driveaway." The first driveaway operations were usually to areas within 100 miles of the factory. Dealers would send employees, family members, or anyone else who could drive to pick up the autos at the factory door. They would return, driving in groups called convoys or caravans. Eventually, driveaway companies became quite sophisticated, with some of them delivering up to 100 autos each day.

In 1914, Frank J. Boutell worked for General Motors' Buick Motor Division in Flint, Michigan. One of his duties was to release the new Buicks to the driveaway drivers who came calling daily. In what might be considered a conflict of interest today, he organized a company that provided driveaway service to dealers in Michigan and Ohio. He was able to retain his position at Buick while directing the operation of his new company, the F. J. Boutell Company. His company grew

Another roadster-cab truck. Information supplied with this photo said "1926 Cadillac" but does it refer to the tractor, the covered autos, or both? Cadillac did produce commercial chassis at this time.

These 1929 Chevrolets have just been unloaded from the boxcars in the background. Note the absence of bumpers. In many cases, the bumpers were considered accessories, to be installed later or left off, depending on customer preference. *JATCO*

This 1928 GMC hauled four cars, two on each deck. It was built and owned by University Overland Express of Cambridge, Massachusetts. This company later became part of the giant East Coast Ford hauler, Nu Car Carriers.

quickly, later serving most of Ohio and even parts of Pennsylvania and New York.

In most cases, driveaway was less expensive than rail and involved much less transit time. In the late 1920s, driveaway companies were delivering autos to destinations as far as 1,000 miles from the factories. In addition to savings in time and money, some driveaway companies advertised that their drivers "scientifically broke in" the new autos they delivered. Later, truckers or haulaway companies would claim the opposite. They saved the important first miles for the owners.

Truck transport of autos was rare before World War I and it would be several more years before truckaway would be a contender for auto haulaway business. During World War I, the truck proved its usefulness in Europe and America. After America's entry into the war in 1917, the railroads were so busy transporting for the war effort they actually encouraged farmers to utilize trucks to help move produce to markets. Freight shipments of less than a full rail carload were also referred to truckers. However, more and better roads would be required for trucking to have a larger part in America's transport future. In the immediate postwar period, Congress set to work to improve America's highways. In the 1920 session, Congress had before it more than 20 highway bills on which to act. The following year, it passed the Federal Highway Act of 1921, providing for the states and the federal government to create a nationwide road system.

The postwar period also saw auto production reaching new highs. However, the railroads found themselves short of equipment to meet the demand. Driveaway was one alternative, but for long-distance shipments, other forms of transport evolved. In and around the Great Lakes, steamship companies moved autos from Michigan's ports east to Buffalo and Cleveland. To the west, Milwaukee, Duluth, and Green Bay also received steamship shipments. In addition to local driveaway companies, some of the Michigan-based companies opened branches in these cities to deliver the autos from the ports to their final destinations. Alternate methods of transport were needed in the winter months when the Great Lakes were frozen over. On the West Coast, coastal steamers shipped cars into Washington and Oregon from assembly plants in California. Upon reaching their destination ports, these vehicles were forwarded to the dealers by rail, driveaway, and later, truckaway. In later years, barges transported autos down America's inland waterways.

Prior to World War I, Ford Motor Company began to establish a nationwide network of regional assembly plants. Its studies revealed that the parts necessary to build 26 Model Ts could be transported in the same rail car space as four completed automobiles. The savings in freight costs enabled Ford to produce and sell

Three of Contract Cartage's trucks loaded and ready to leave Lansing, Michigan. Contract Cartage was a GM carrier founded in 1926 by Frank Newman and Edward Rice. *NATA*

This 1929 GMC is pulling a six-car, two-deck trailer. The autos on the upper deck were loaded by means of an elevator at the rear of the unit. Note the very short wheelbase tractor required with this combination.

automobiles for less. One of Ford's earliest plants was in Cambridge, Massachusetts. Lester J. Lishon, Sr., began a long relationship with Ford by hauling first components, then completed autos out of that plant in 1922. His original company was called Transportation Contractors, Inc. In 1926, he changed the name to University Overland Express, and in 1929 it became the exclusive carrier out of Ford's new plant in Somerville, Massachusetts. Later, the Lishon family would come to own Nu Car Carriers, a major Ford carrier in the East.

Ford also had a plant in Chicago that began building Model Ts in 1924. Using a flat-bed truck and trailer, Alexander S. H. Bender began hauling autos from this plant to Chicago area dealers. As his business increased, he needed capital to buy additional equipment. To raise the money, he sold the dealers he served shares in his company, Dealers Transport. Bender's company was limited to using trailers that transported only two or three autos because of Illinois' railroad-inspired restrictions on trailer lengths. Dealers Transport remained a

W. R. Arthur's first haulaway trucks were 1929 GMCs like this. This simple trailer could transport three or four autos. Note the marker lights on the cab roof and the small rearview mirror. *Janesville Auto Transport*

"You'll be the first driver." One of the primary reasons that dealers and car buyers preferred truckaway was that the owner was able to put the "break-in" mileage on the vehicle. The cars and truck are 1929 Chevrolets, on a Whitehead & Kales (W&K) trailer. *W&K*

Ford carrier for many years, serving the Midwest and some areas of the East.

Other manufacturers also opened regional assembly plants. The first Chevrolet autos came off GM's Janesville, Wisconsin, plant in mid-1923. The plant had previously produced farm tractors and Samson trucks. Arthur and Company, successor to Arthur and Black, became one of Janesville's first carriers, initially delivering autos by driveaway.

By the mid-1920s, trucks and roads were improved to a point where intercity trucking was available in many areas. Balloon tires, available on autos for some time, were perfected for use on trucks and trailers. Along with an improved ride, they permitted higher highway speeds. At the same time, driveaway companies began experimenting with trucks and trailers as a way to increase productivity. The earliest pieces of auto transport equipment were flat-bed trailers on which three or four autos were loaded end to end. Since it was commonplace to transport four autos in a railroad boxcar, truckers attempted to offer competitive rates by standardizing on four autos as a transport load. These early trailers were up to 50 feet long, and the resulting tractor-trailer combination lengths were 60 feet. While legal in many states at that time, these units were difficult to handle, especially in congested areas. With increased automobile use, public sentiment and pressure from railroad lobbyists brought state highway laws that reduced trailers to an average 50-foot overall length. Railroad-minded legislators believed that these restrictions would eliminate the four-car payload and force haulaway companies out of business. The answer was equipment that tilted the autos on ramps and permitted four of them to be loaded in the same space or less. In some cases, an auto would extend forward over the cab of the tractor, while on other types of trailers, autos were inclined on ramps in a saw-tooth fashion, with some autos carried at precarious angles.

Double-deck trailers also appeared in limited numbers in the late 1920s. Automobile Transport, Inc., a Michigan company, could transport six autos on each of its double-deck trailers. These heavier loads required larger tractors and it was necessary to shorten the tractor in every conceivable way to comply with state length regulations. This type of equipment was heavy, complicated, and expensive. The average carrier at the time could not justify the additional investment, even though more revenue-producing units could be transported.

Much of the early transport equipment was home-built or improvised by the carriers themselves. There were several companies offering haulaway trailers commercially, especially in the Detroit area. One of these companies was the Whitehead & Kales Company, whose first offerings, in 1927, were single-deck trailers. W&K later developed state-of-the-art double-deck transporters, which it called Tu-Deck transporters.

Driveaway accounted for 27 percent of new vehicle deliveries in 1929, the year that the stock market crashed, triggering the depression of the 1930s. However, a new era of automobile transportation was beginning. Many of the original driveaway companies like Boutell, Arthur, and Howard Sober, Inc. (Sober), began to offer truckaway service. Dealers who elected to use the new and more expensive service received timely delivery of factory-fresh autos at their front door. Driveaway and rail transport would continue to be the primary auto transport methods for many more years. However, truckaway's roots were firmly planted, and the business would continue to grow in every part of the country.

Rear view of a W&K single-deck trailer. Note the absence of taillights or even reflectors and the extreme rear overhang. *W&K*

CHAPTER 2

The 1930s

Depression and Regulation

The deepest days of the depression were 1931 and 1932. Automobile sales dropped 29 percent in 1931 and another 42.5 percent in 1932. Production was at its lowest since 1918. Massive layoffs occurred in the supporting industries, including the automobile transporters. As a result, competition between transporters increased as they searched for additional work to replace the lost shipments.

A government program called the National Recovery Act (NRA) included road building and repairs and helped create work for many unemployed Americans. Route 66, between Chicago and Los Angeles, was completed and opened to traffic in 1932. For the next 25 years, America's Interstate Highway System would consist of two- and three-lane concrete roads similar to Route 66 and the Lincoln Highway, completed four years previous. Individually, states passed more restrictions on trucks to lessen the effects of heavy loads on road surfaces. By 1932, solid rubber tires were outlawed on most hard surface roads. In addition, taxes were levied in the form of motor fuel tax, weight-based license fees and permits, and some states imposed a ton-mile tax on cargoes. Despite these regulations and taxes, trucking increased in popularity. Shippers and receivers both benefited from the door-to-door service and quick delivery that trucking offered.

In August 1933, Walter Carey, president of Motorcar Transport, presided over a meeting of representatives from 16 auto transport companies. This meeting resulted in the creation of the National Automobile Transporters Association (NATA). One of NATA's earliest concerns was the varying truck size restrictions between states. Their goal was to get the 45-foot tractor and semitrailer combination approved for use in every state. Unfortunately, that goal would not be attained for many years.

By loading the autos on an incline, this trailer is able to transport four Model A Fords and still comply with the shorter length limits imposed in the 1930s. The tractor is a late 1920s GMC. The Model A Ford succeeded the Model T in 1928 and remained in production through 1931.

Compare the overall length of this load of four 1930 Dodges with the load of Model A Fords. The tractor pulling this load is also a 1930 Dodge.

This two-ton Dodge tractor with "penthouse" sleeper hauled new cars from Detroit, Michigan, to Holdrege, Nebraska. In 1931, the 2,000-mile round trip took 80 driving hours.

The Ray Carr Transit Company operated a fleet of 12 lightweight Kenworth trucks and long single-deck trailers in the Northwest in the 1930s. In 1932, the company name was changed to the Interstate Transit Company; later it became part of the Convoy Company. *Ackroyd Photography Inc.*

The growth of the trucking industry, in particular the auto transporters, did not go unnoticed by the railroads. The Interstate Commerce Commission (ICC) had begun regulating their activities before the turn of the century. Although the railroads were successful in getting trucking regulated in several states, it was not until 1928 that Congress would propose that the ICC impose federal regulations on trucking. The Federal Motor Carrier Act of 1932 gave the ICC the power to regulate interstate trucking, although the ICC would take three years to formulate the regulations which would become the Motor Carrier Act of 1935. Opposition to the act came from the automobile and truck manufacturers and other shippers who feared increased freight rates. Support for passage came from the states looking for federal minimum safety and insurance standards. The railroads also lobbied for passage of the act, which would make their competitors subject to economic regulations similar to those under which they operated.

The Motor Carrier Act of 1935 became effective on April 1, 1936, and affected all carriers engaged in interstate transport. Those carriers that could show proof of operation in a certain geographic area in the period of March to June of 1935 were given grandfather certificates and permits for rights in those areas. Later, carriers would be required to formally apply for new authority, with supporting statements from prospective shippers and subject to the protest of other carriers claiming the ability to handle the traffic. Carriers were also required to file as private, common, or contract carriers.

Four 1932 Chrysler Imperials loaded and ready to move out. Note the trunk, which was an optional accessory, and side-mount spare tire on the front auto. The other autos have been shipped with spare wheels but no tires. The tractor is a Dodge G-80.

(See sidebar.) The status of many of the grandfather carriers would not formally be resolved for two years or more. Nevertheless, they made their rate filings on April 1, 1936, and thereafter considered themselves private, common, or contract carriers, according to their choice.

Certificates and permits were issued to the carriers and specified the type of commodities they could haul, the type of service that could be rendered, the routes over which operations could be conducted, the points that could be served, and the classes of shippers to

Here's the rear view of the Imperial load. Note that the auto's rear wheels are placed in a dolly that travels on the trailer's upper siderails. Since these cars were not front-wheel drive, they would need to be pushed on and pulled off the trailer.

This 1933 Dodge rig is one of the first Illinois specials built by W&K. Two 1933 Dodge autos are riding on the truck, while two more are carried on the trailer. Square Deal Cartage was primarily a Chrysler carrier. *NATA*

In 1931, Chrysler Corporation introduced "Floating Power," thick rubber motor mounts that isolated engine vibrations from the frame and body. Automobile Shippers, Inc., another Chrysler carrier, promoted it on the sides of its transport trailers.

Fully enclosed trailers have been used to a limited extent since the 1930s. In addition to protecting the cargo, they allowed plenty of space for advertising. Note the "power brakes" warning. *Phillip Baumgarten*

which service could be rendered. Although formerly, an interstate carrier specializing in one type of service could switch to other types as business conditions justified, this practice was now forbidden without ICC consent. Since auto transport equipment was not suitable for hauling general freight, this was not a major concern for the auto transporters.

By 1934, recovery from the depression was under way and automobile and truck production was increasing. Across the country, more dealers were requesting truckaway as the method of delivering their new cars. Many of the carriers that would later become industry giants had their start in the 1930s.

Convoy Company was started in Portland, Oregon, in 1930, hauling Fords received there by steamship from the Ford plant in Richmond, California. Originally called Consolidated Convoy, it was part of Consolidated Freight Lines. Starting with 11 Ford Model AA trucks and trailers, it hauled to points as far as 600 miles inland. Convoy would go on to become a major West Coast carrier, eventually becoming part of the Ryder system in the 1980s.

Another long-time Ford carrier was E&L Transport. Founded in Michigan in 1932, it soon expanded into Indiana and Ohio. E&L continues today as a major Ford carrier in those areas and beyond.

In Hamel, Illinois, Albert and Arnold Cassens were in the automobile business with their father, George. Not wishing to wait two weeks for rail delivery of the Hudsons, Dodges, and Plymouths they sold, they would travel to Detroit by bus and drive their new cars home. Using tow bars, the two brothers could transport four cars per trip. In 1933 they purchased a two-ton Dodge truck and a Mechanical Handling Systems (MHS) auto transport trailer for $1,850. In September of that year, the truck was put into service and one driver was now able to return with four automobiles. When not busy hauling their own vehicles, they offered their service to other dealers in the Illinois area. By 1935, their fleet had grown to six rigs, all Dodges. Although Cassens Transport has always hauled vehicles for other manufacturers, it established a special relationship with Chrysler that would benefit both firms in the years to come.

Even though the auto manufacturers had established regional assembly plants in various parts of the country, the Michigan, Ohio, and Indiana area remained the center of major auto production. There was a great deal of competition for the haulaway business in this area, resulting at times, in many carriers serving a single shipper. The number of carriers serving Chrysler was particularly large because of that firm's distribution system. Chrysler allowed its dealers or distributors to contract with carriers for shipment of their vehicles. This was unlike the situation at Chevrolet and other shippers, who arranged and prepaid all outbound shipments. This limited their number of haulaway carriers to one or two, while other manufacturers like Chrysler were dealing with many.

This was W&K's auto transport trailer lineup for 1933 and 1934. The three-car unit is especially interesting, in that the lower auto is mounted on a turntable.

Anchor Motor Freight was able to transport four 1934 Chevrolets and remain legal by loading one auto over the cab and using a three-car trailer. The cover on the first auto protected it from low-hanging tree branches.

In an attempt to simplify working with multiple carriers, auto manufacturers used "releasing companies," whose job it was to get the correct vehicle from the factory gate and deliver it to the haulaway carrier. They would accept the vehicle and supporting paperwork and, for a small fee, forward the vehicles to the driveaway company, haulaway company, or to the outbound rail yard. In some cases they stored vehicles in their own yards, where carriers would call for them, or they might transport the vehicles to the carriers' yards,

Four 1934 Nash autos on one of Arthur's Illinois specials. The rear-most axle on the Chevrolet truck is the "dolly" added to comply with Illinois law. *JATCO*

where outbound loads were built. Some of the larger carriers also performed releasing operations. Sober handled the releasing for Oldsmobile in Lansing, Michigan, for many years and remained one of Oldsmobile's primary carriers until the 1970s.

Although truckaway had grown in popularity in the 1930s, driveaway and railroad still accounted for a large number of shipments. Rail equipment was improved with the introduction of the 40-foot boxcar equipped with the Evans Auto Loader, which accommodated four automobiles, two on movable ramps and two on the floor. Loading time was reduced to 30 minutes or less, and unloading time was improved with wider door openings. Large trucks were shipped in 50-foot

boxcars called "nailers" because the trucks were supported by lumber nailed in place. These units sometimes had doors on each end, enabling vehicles to be driven straight in. The Auto Loader and nailer would remain in service in many railroads through the 1950s. For vehicles produced in some factories, rail was the only economical method of shipment to outlying areas of the country.

Where truckaway was possible, variations of the flat single-deck trailers of the 1920s continued in use well into the 1930s. Able to be loaded and unloaded quickly, they were preferred by the Detroit area releasing companies and carriers doing local deliveries. While the use of these long trailers was still legal in Michigan, they were considered "overlength" in many other areas. The 50-foot overall length restriction in effect in many states previously was reduced to 40 feet or even less. This necessitated the use of double-deck trailers. The most common double-deck trailers were four-car models, but in some areas, length or weight restrictions permitted only three-car loads. The double-deck trailer was continuously perfected in the 1930s until the models in use at the end of the decade were pretty much state of the art for the next twenty years.

In the western states, length and height restrictions were not as critical as in the East. Although the tractor and double-deck trailer combination was used in the West, western four-car rigs tended to be lighter weight single-deck units. Much of this early equipment was shop-built and the truck and full trailer was a popular setup in the West.

The state of Illinois presented a major problem for auto transporters operating there. Under pressure from that state's powerful railroad lobby, the state legislature

This type of trailer, on which only the lower deck was enclosed, was sometimes called a "tank" because it resembled a fuel tanker. The tractor is a 1934 Ford BB-13.

Where length or weight was a factor, lighter, shorter three-car rigs were used. This 1933 Ford tractor is ready to move out with three 1933 or 1934 Ford cars. Again, the tops of the cars are protected from low tree limbs. This was especially important in the summer months, when the trees were heavy with leaves.

This is a different type of three-car trailer, in which the front car is loaded with the trailer unhooked from the tractor. The other two autos are loaded from the rear.

An early single-axle, two-deck trailer with a load of 1934 Chevrolets. The tractor is a 1934 White belonging to Arner Convoy of Buffalo, New York. *The White Motor Company*

The Mack Jr. was a product of a mid-1930s joint venture with Reo, which gave Mack a line of light- and medium-duty trucks to sell. This 1936 COE model was quite rare. The load is made up of 1936 Dodges. *Phillip Baumgarten*

passed a law limiting tractor and trailer combination lengths to 35 feet. The carriers were struggling to keep their length within 40 feet elsewhere and it seemed impossible that a four-car trailer could be made any shorter. Two- and three-car rigs could comply, but the transporters needed the fourth car to compete with the railroads' four-car rate. Eventually, the trailer builders and transporters found a loophole in the law. Illinois' law allowed a truck and full trailer, as opposed to a tractor and semitrailer, to have an overall length of 40 feet. A piece of equipment known as an "Illinois special" was designed. On this rig, two autos were transported on the truck, one above the cab and one on a deck behind. Two more autos were carried on a short double-deck trailer connected to the truck by means of a drawbar. This outfit was purely a "law compliance" rather than a practical piece of equipment. It was first built in 1933 and was more complicated to load and more hazardous to operate than the conventional tractor

Arthur was one of two carriers working out of Chevrolet's Janesville, Wisconsin, plant in 1936. This line-up of Illinois specials is ready to move out on January 5, 1936.

and semitrailer. Illinois officials ruled that the trailer was a semitrailer and did not comply with their statutes. While a full trailer supports the weight of its load on two or more axles, a portion of the cargo weight on a semitrailer is transferred to the truck or tractor, in this case by the drawbar. To bring the Illinois special into compliance, it became necessary to add a two-wheel dolly under the drawbar, making it technically a full trailer. When operating outside Illinois the dolly could be raised and chained up, preventing unnecessary tire wear. The Illinois special was the only type of four-car outfit permitted in Illinois until after World War II. However, the carriers were able to get permission to eliminate the dolly after demonstrating that the unit could be operated safely without it. The Illinois specials were sometimes called "bailers" or "banana wagons." The streamlined versions that appeared in the late 1930s were called "comets."

Kentucky was another state where auto transporters had to contend with railroad-inspired regulations. Motor carriers there were limited to a 30-foot length and a 7,000-pound cargo weight, which was less than the weight of three autos. The law especially affected the carriers at Ford's plant in Louisville. The truckers were required to leave there with two-car loads bound for areas

This is a West Coast combination operated by Consolidated Convoy in 1936. Part of Consolidated Freight Lines, this company later became the Convoy Company. The 1935 Ford truck is loaded with 1936 Ford vehicles. *Convoy Company*

Another load of 1936 Chevrolets on an Arthur Illinois special. Note the side-mount spare tire and that the autos on the upper decks have been covered. The drivers appear to be fairly well dressed for loading automobiles.

Dodge did not build COE models until 1940. However, outside body builders converted Dodge chassis to a cab-over configuration. One of the most popular conversions was this one, built by the Montpelier Body Works.

This rear view of the Montpelier Dodge shows how the loading skids were positioned for loading or unloading the top deck of the Mechanical Handling Systems (MHS) trailer. In actual practice, the lower deck was loaded first and unloaded last.

across the state line where three- and four-car loads could be rebuilt. Three- and four-car loads coming into Kentucky also had to unload before entering the state and transfer their loads to two-car rigs for delivery. Fortunately, before 1940, the weight restrictions were changed and four-car rigs were then permitted in Kentucky.

In the late 1930s, Pennsylvania, and later West Virginia, outlawed two-deck transporters, claiming that they were unsafe. The NATA and the ICC went to court and fought the ruling, with the contention that Pennsylvania was impeding interstate transport. Pennsylvania responded that it had ultimate authority over the size of vehicles operated in the state. The Supreme Court ruled in Pennsylvania's favor, although in the 1940s both Pennsylvania and West Virginia allowed two-deck equipment back on their highways.

These 1937 DeSotos are being prepared for rail shipment. Note the autos in the background that have already been loaded in a boxcar and are being secured for travel.

Smoother riding pneumatic tires and fully en-closed cabs helped create a better working environment for the truck driver of the 1930s. Hydraulic brakes, sometimes power-assisted, and trailer brakes, vacuum or electric, made operation of long combinations safer. However, compliance with overall length restrictions continued to be a problem. To solve this problem, truck operators began to look back at the design of the early motor trucks.

The first trucks were designed so that the driver sat above the front wheels and over or in front of the engine. In the 1920s, the trend was to place the driver behind the engine. The trucks of the early 1930s looked much like the contemporary autos, with a long hood. In an attempt to reduce the length, truck makers again began to experiment with cab-over engine (COE) models. Autocar, Mack, and Sterling began offering COEs as early as 1934.

The auto transporters favored lower-priced tractors like Fords, Dodges, or Chevrolets that were not offered as factory-built COEs. Montpelier Body Works in Ohio and other truck body builders began offering COE conversions based on these medium-duty chassis. In 1937, GM introduced its F-series COEs, which were actually short-hood cab-forward models. Ford followed in 1938 with a similar factory-built model. Dodge continued to offer the Montpelier cab until 1940, when it too, began building COEs in-house. Using COE tractors, the auto transporters were able to use the four-car double-deck transport trailer in almost every state except Illinois.

W. R. Arthur appeared to be quite satisfied with electric trailer brakes in this ad dating from 1937. Vacuum and air brakes would soon replace the electric trailer brake.

This is the front view of the rig that appeared in the Warner Electric Brake ad. The tractor is a 1937 GMC "snub-nose," as cab-overs of this type were sometimes called. Note the single tires on the axles of this MHS trailer. This setup enabled the rig to have four braking axles and permitted a lower deck floor. The autos are 1937 Chevrolets.

This is a W&K trailer and Montpelier Dodge operated by Baker Driveaway Company. Note how close this trailer is coupled to the tractor, and the size of the 1938 Packards on board. *W&K*

Rear inside view of a W&K trailer with single tires. Note that vehicles can be driven between the wheels rather than up and over them, as is the case on a trailer with dual wheels. *W&K*

At some assembly plants, automobile bodies were built at other locations and trucked to the plant for final assembly. These 1937 Chrysler bodies are en route to the final assembly plant, pulled by a 1937 Dodge tractor.

Another close-coupled rig, this one a 1937 Chevrolet operated by Boutell. Note the absence of bumpers on these Buicks. They will be installed at the dealership. This trailer is a Francis, built in Detroit, Michigan. *F. J. Boutell Driveaway*

M&G Convoy also used Francis trailers to transport autos in the Northeast. These 1938 Dodge cars have been transported to Buffalo, New York, from Detroit via steamship. M&G will now deliver them to their final destination.

COMMON OR CONTRACT CARRIER?

When the motor carriers applied for their ICC certificate, whether a "grandfather" filing or subsequent application, they were required to elect to become private, common, or contract carriers. There were advantages and disadvantages to each type of service, and the election was usually based on the relationship the carrier had with its shippers.

The private carriers were usually manufacturers or distributors who delivered their products with their own trucks. Under regulation, they could not offer their services to other shippers on a for-hire basis. There were very few instances of auto transporters operating as private carriers in interstate commerce.

Common carriers were free to serve all shippers within their prescribed area at the rates filed with the ICC. When a particular auto maker's production and resulting shipments were down, the common carriers could use their equipment to serve other manufacturers. Most of the auto transporters who were common carriers became members of NATA and participated in rates filed by that association. Although their freight rates were less than those charged by contract carriers, the common carriers enjoyed more freedom to switch shippers and could rely on a larger customer base.

Contract carriers were limited to serving only a few carriers (sometimes only one) with whom they had entered into contract. This provided the shipper with a dedicated fleet and enabled it to control, to some extent, the activities of the carrier. Chevrolet was one of the first auto makers to employ contract carriers. By doing so, Chevrolet was able to prepay shipments and limit the number of carriers with whom it did business. The carrier benefited by receiving a higher freight rate and a guarantee that its work was not going to be given to another carrier. However, if the manufacturer experienced a strike or production cutback, the carrier was left without another source of freight.

One auto transporter, Arthur and Company, applied for both common and contract carrier status within substantially the same territory. Arthur was under contract to Chevrolet, transporting cars from its Janesville, Wisconsin, plant. Arthur also had driveaway and truckaway operations in Wisconsin and Kentucky that were better suited to common carrier status. In 1938, the ICC did issue Arthur both contract and common carrier certificates. This was the only instance in the auto transport field when both types of authority with duplicating rights were issued to a single company. Arthur's common carrier work in Kentucky involved truckaway operations from Ford's Louisville plant, which was frowned on by Chevrolet. In an effort to appease Chevrolet, Arthur split his company into W. R. Arthur, a contract carrier in Janesville, Wisconsin, which he managed, and ARCO Carriers, a common carrier based in Chicago and administered by his wife, Hazel. The ARCO operation became a major transporter of Nash (later American Motors Corporation) and other automobiles.

Deregulation in the 1980s eliminated many of the differences between the common and contract carrier. Today, even private carriers are able to haul other manufacturer products for hire.

A Montpelier Dodge owned by Automobile Shippers, Inc., of Detroit. Note the condition of the tires on this rig, including the spare on the MHS trailer. The decals with an "M" superimposed on the map of the United States indicate that this vehicle is subject to inspection by the Markle Company. The company observed the operation of trucking fleets and reported their findings to the operator's home office.

This three-car rig was built to comply with the restrictive laws of Kentucky. The 1937 Chevrolet tractor has been shortened so much that the wheels are almost at the back of the cab. The two-car trailer is similar to those used on Illinois specials. *NATA*

These 1939 Chevrolets are being loaded on a W&K trailer. Loading ramps like this, used at the assembly plants and loading yards, were more stable than the portable skids carried on the rigs. The bottom cars have already been loaded and secured. *NATA*

Anchor Motor Freight operated this 1939 Chevrolet COE. The trucks on top of the semienclosed trailer are also 1939s. At this time, Anchor primarily hauled for Chevrolet, and its trailers proclaim Chevrolet's boast of being "First in Value, First in Sales." *Anchor Motor Freight*

In 1939, Dodge introduced a diesel engine, based on its six-cylinder gasoline design. The engine was not reintroduced after World War II. At least one found its way into the J. M. Propst, Jr. auto transport fleet.

A brand new 1939 Chevrolet with an MHS Illinois special trailer owned by Arthur. Note that Arthur continued to use the dolly, which technically made the unit a full trailer.

CHAPTER 3

The 1940s

World War II and Peace

The developments in automobile technology of the 1930s resulted in autos in 1940 that barely resembled those produced 15 years earlier. Manufacturers were now stressing styling and driver comforts in their advertising. The first fully automatic transmission, the Hydra-Matic, was available in the 1940 Oldsmobile, and Chrysler offered a semiautomatic transmission in several of its models. Exposed running boards were gone and the latest styling included headlights fared into the front fenders. More Americans than ever could afford and were buying new autos. They were traveling the nation's highways in record numbers and stopping at gas stations, diners, and motels. The nation's first "super highway," the Pennsylvania Turnpike, opened its first 160 miles of roadway to traffic on October 1, 1940.

By early 1941, war had already been raging in Europe for two years. Many Americans feared it would only be a short time until the United States would be directly involved. In 1940, many automobile and truck manufacturers were awarded contracts to build government vehicles, some of which went to our future allies via Lend-Lease. Additional contracts for vehicles and war material were awarded to them in 1941. Following the Japanese attack at Pearl Harbor on December 7, 1941, the United States was at war with Japan and Germany. Within in a matter of days, America's industries mobilized for war production. Automobile production was curtailed and the final civilian autos came off the assembly lines in early 1942. Stocks of vehicles in dealer and manufacturer inventories were frozen by the government and could only be released with government authorization.

Although 1940 had been a record year, with more than four million vehicles delivered by haulaway and driveaway, without automobiles to transport and with

Dodge's COE, new for 1940, was built in-house. Power was from Dodge's 228-cubic inch, 92-horsepower L-head six-cylinder engine. The 1940 Plymouths are riding on an MHS trailer.

Rail transport remained popular in the 1940s. These workers are securing 1940 Chrysler vehicles in an Evans Auto Loader boxcar. Note the autos in the raised position, supported on movable ramps. *American Automobile Manufacturers Assoc.*

Motorcar Transport Company operated this 1940 GMC COE truck and Illinois special trailer. Primarily a GM carrier, Motorcar became one of America's largest auto transport firms before World War II. Note the unusual five-lug wheels on the rig. *Phillip Baumgarten*

many of their employees going off to serve in the armed forces, the future of the auto transporters looked dismal. To support the war effort, the NATA and the management teams of many haulaway companies reacted quickly. Executives such as Cap Boutell of Boutell, Lloyd Lawson of E&L Transport, Gene Cassarol of Automobile Shippers, Howard Sober, and others displayed the ingenuity that had made them leaders in the auto transport industry. They met with the military chiefs in Washington, D.C., and offered their companies' services. Shortly afterward, their representatives met with military traffic expediting officers and developed plans for transporting war materiel.

Except for the hauling of light trucks and Jeeps, the auto transport equipment needed extensive modifications and even rebuilding to transport war materiel.

Much of this equipment had to be stripped to the axles and rebuilt in various configurations.

In the Northwest, Convoy shut down its operations for the duration of the war, while the Ford carrier in California, Hadley Auto Transport, contracted to transport fighters and bombers from California aircraft plants to Texas. Hadley also hauled aviation fuel from Montebello to the Los Angeles harbor, rubber wing tanks from Los Angeles to Sacramento, and airplane engines from Sacramento to San Bernardino, California.

Another California carrier, H and M Truckaway, had been hauling autos out of Studebaker's assembly plant in Los Angeles since the mid-1930s. Before World War II, it had been one of the first truckaway companies to use six-car equipment. With no autos to haul for the war years, H and M secured a government

The lightweight Ford 9N farm tractor was introduced in 1939. This photo, taken in 1940, shows seven 9Ns loaded on a specially built 1940 Ford COE and MHS Illinois special type trailer operated by E&L Transport.

For economic reasons, two-car rigs like this 1940 Chevrolet leased to Arthur were limited to use for local deliveries. The autos are also 1940 Chevrolets. *Ted Ahrens*

Ford restyled its COE models for the 1941 model year with a grille that was similar to the one used on the conventional cabs. E&L Transport, Ford's transporter in Michigan and Indiana, used Ford trucks exclusively in the 1930s and 1940s. *E&L Transport*

defense contract to haul LP gas to the military installations in California and Nevada. Its gas transport fleet grew to nine rigs of various makes, including Autocars, GMCs and Studebakers. Before the war's end, H and M's ownership changed and the name was changed to B and H Truckaway. After the war, it again transported Studebakers, using trucks assembled in its own shops. Later, a fleet of Reo Gold Comets replaced the home-built specials.

Some transporters, because of their locations, were unable to find government work for the war years. In Wisconsin, the Chevrolet plant and the Fisher Body plant were converted to ammunition production, all of which moved out by rail and general freight carriers. For a short time, Arthur leased some of its equipment to contractors doing construction work at Camp McCoy, in nearby Sparta, Wisconsin. It also leased its office fa-

cilities to a local bus company, but Arthur remained inactive for the remainder of the war.

Cassens, in Illinois, was also left with a fleet of auto transporters and nothing to haul. With no new trucks available for civilian operators, they were easily able to sell their tractors to general freight carriers. Shortly before the war, Cassens had purchased a large piece of real estate on which they were storing stocks of new autos frozen by the federal government. Rather than cut their trailers up for scrap, they used this property to store 28 of them for the duration of the war.

On the East Coast, Anchor Motor Freight was a contract carrier hauling Chevrolets before hostilities shut down auto production. Anchor was able to utilize a limited number of its trucks and trailers to move lifeboats and rubber products between Ohio and the East Coast ports.

This Consolidated Convoy unit with a load of 1941 Fords was a one-of-a-kind rig. The bottom car on the trailer was mounted on a turntable that rotated to the right for unloading. The tractor is a holdover from the 1935–1937 period. *Ackroyd Photography Inc.*

Along with government-imposed gasoline and tire rationing, Americans were urged to use mass transportation as much as possible. Since the nation's bus builders were no longer building coaches for civilian use, buses were in extremely short supply; particularly those needed to transport defense workers. One solution was to convert unused auto transport trailers into passenger trailers by enclosing the sides and installing seating. Some of the converted trailers remained in use for a short period after the war, until buses became available again.

The Motor Convoy, a carrier in Georgia, converted its rigs into sleeping cars for the highway transport of troops in this country. After conversion, the rigs were

Covered for protection from low-hanging tree limbs, these 1941 Pontiacs have been loaded on an MHS trailer. Unlike the earlier MHS trailers shown previously, this one has a single axle with dual wheels and, most likely, vacuum brakes. The Boutell tractor is a 1941 Dodge.

purchased and operated by the military. At the war's end, the Motor Convoy was able to repurchase and reconvert this equipment to haul autos.

Most of the wheeled vehicles produced for the war came from manufacturers in the Detroit area such as Dodge and GMC. In addition to using Detroit truck-away operators such as F. J. Boutell and Automobile Shippers to move these units, many more moved via driveaway. At times, the need for driveaway drivers far exceeded the number of regular drivers available. The driveaway operators were forced to rely on volunteers from the American Red Cross, office of Civil Defense, the Civil Air Patrol, school teachers, police and fire officers, and other civilian organizations to do the driving.

In addition to driveaway operations, F. J. Boutell's wartime work was extensive and varied. Much of its equipment was converted to haul specialized materiel. One of its most ambitious projects was transporting the then-top secret radar equipment, valued at about a half-million dollars per load. In order to transport this special cargo, the haulaway trailers were stripped down and rebuilt into van-type units that could be locked and secured with a Signal Corps seal. Two drivers were assigned to each load and a sleeping compartment was built into the front of the trailer. When on the move, these trucks carried an official document signed by a high-ranking Signal Corps officer, which certified that the unit was on an exclusive lease to the U.S. Army. It further stated that the unit had the same status as a government vehicle and that the Signal Corps seal must not be molested by anyone, including law enforcement.

Another Detroit area carrier that was involved in specialized transport operations was E&L Transport. In cooperation with the Army, it developed transporters to haul B-24 Liberator bombers from the huge plant in

The trucks in this lineup of 1940 and 1941 Dodges are operated by Automobile Shippers, Inc. The second and fifth trucks in line are 1941s, identifiable by the small cowl lights added that year.

Streamlined Illinois specials like this MHS model were sometimes called "comets." Note the dolly is no longer being used on this W. R. Arthur rig. The truck is a 1940, and the autos are 1942 Chevrolets.

New front-end styling graced the 1941 Chevrolet trucks. This MHS trailer is loaded with 1942 Chevrolet cars. Note Chevrolet's new motto, "The Finest Chevrolet of All Time for the Service of America." Could Chevrolet's ad people have foreseen the coming world conflict?

The U.S. Government purchased large numbers of vehicles in 1940 and 1941. Many were militarized commercial vehicles like these 1 1/2-ton Fords with military type cargo beds. Auto Convoy is the operator of this rig adapted to transport large vehicles. *NATA*

Willow Run, Michigan, to final assembly plants in Texas and Oklahoma. One hundred trailers 65 feet long and 12 1/2 feet high were built by MHS in Detroit. Each trailer could haul the wings or fuselage for a B-24. In fact, everything to build a complete bomber except the engines was transported in two trailers. Pulling these trailers were special two-engine COE tractors called Dearborn Dual Drives or Thorco Dual Motors. Of the 100 of these units built, E&L operated 96 for the army, and four were sold to civilian operators. When hooked up to the trailers and loaded, these rigs were 77 feet long. Obviously their routes had to be carefully laid out, as they were the biggest combinations on the road at the time. In addition to the Michigan-to-Texas route, these rigs were also used on the West Coast, possibly by Hadley Auto Transport.

Much of this specialized equipment, especially the trailers used to transport aircraft components, was oversized. In addition, carriers were required to operate in areas beyond which their ICC certificates authorized. The urgency of the war traffic, however, caused an administrative order to be issued allowing a relaxation of rules and emergency temporary authority was granted by the ICC when military traffic suddenly required it. Temporary authority grants were issued for a specified length of time, and at the close of hostilities the commission canceled all of these special rights.

In 1945, the end of the war seemed in sight and the auto makers began to contemplate civilian automobile production. The auto transporters also began to prepare for production to resume. Most of the equipment that had been in use during the war years was nearly or

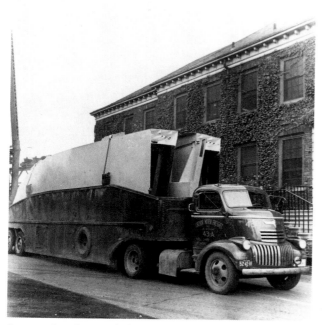

By removing the top deck of an enclosed trailer, Anchor Motor Freight was able to transport oversize loads of war materiel. The COE Chevrolet seen here also received new styling for 1941. *Anchor Motor Freight*

totally worn out. Production of civilian trucks was authorized in late 1944, but only in limited numbers. When the restrictions on civilian sales were relaxed, the number of purchasers greatly exceeded the stocks available. Usable auto transport equipment was scarce as much had been converted for the war effort and trailer manufacturers were unable to get materials to build new trailers. Immediately after the war, steel and rubber were in short supply. In fact, throughout most of the late 1940s, material shortages, labor problems, and strikes plagued America's automotive industry. Most transporters rebuilt all the equipment they could and held on until new trucks and trailers were available.

Cassens still had the 28 transport trailers that it had put into storage in 1942, but no tractors. In Detroit, Chrysler had a field full of Dodge trucks built during the last days of the war. Previously, they were available only to purchasers designated by the government as essential users. Now that civilian sales were again authorized, Cassens approached Chrysler with a request to buy 28 of these trucks. In return, Cassens assured Chrysler the trucks would be available to haul their postwar auto production. When the deal was done, Cassens dragged its old trailers out of storage and reconditioned them. Cassens Transport was back in business with 28 rigs, and its relationship with Chrysler was strengthened.

The amphibious version of the World War II Jeep was built by Ford Motor Company and known as the "GPA." Boutell has extended the top deck of this MHS trailer to accommodate three GPAs. Two more are transported on the bottom deck. The tractor is a 1940 GMC. *F. J. Boutell Driveaway Co.*

An early 1940s Dodge conventional tractor and MHS trailer is transporting antitank gun carriages. It appears that this trailer did not require any modifications for this task. The gun carriages were produced in civilian factories and then shipped to government plants for installation of the gun tube. *F. J. Boutell Driveaway Co.*

This is one of the rigs Boutell used to transport secret radar equipment. The top decks of the auto transport trailer were cut away and replaced with van-type bodywork. The area in the front of the trailer was used as a sleeping compartment. *F. J. Boutell Driveaway Co.*

This pre-war MHS auto transport trailer has been converted into a "sleeper" by the Auto Convoy in Texas. Similar conversions were done by other transporters. Trailers that were converted into busses looked much like this but with a lower roofline. *NATA*

Operated by E&L, this trailer has been specially constructed to transport "flat-face" cowl and chassis units. These are early postwar units, with no chrome or contrasting trim, and probably going to be built into school buses. *Phillip Baumgarten*

In July 1946, the American Trucking Association promoted the benefits of truckaway delivery in this magazine ad. The tractor appears to be an artist's conception of a postwar Chevrolet.

With the exception of the 1946 Studebaker, most automobiles produced in the immediate postwar period were carryover models, similar to the 1942 models. Masses of returning GIs and other Americans who had not had a new car for five years or more created a seller's market for new autos. Many buyers who wanted one of the modern-styled Studebakers or the new Kaiser often had to settle for another manufacturer's carryover model simply because it was the only auto available. Auto sales in the postwar period were limited only by the number that each manufacturer could produce. The postwar material shortages and labor problems also affected automobile production. Chrysler, Ford, and GM did not offer completely restyled models until the 1949 model year, when the seller's market was cooling off.

Like the autos, the trucks built in 1946 were similar to the prewar models. The Big Three introduced restyled and improved truck models for the 1948 model year, one year before they would introduce restyled autos. Chevrolet's new truck was called the Advance-Design series and a similar medium-duty GMC was also produced. Ford's new truck was the first of the F-series, while Dodge's 1948 models were known as the B-1-models. All three makers reintroduced COE models preferred by the auto carriers, but Dodge's 1948 model retained the prewar styling. It was updated in 1949, with the introduction of the B-2-models. Dodge

Traffic Transport Engineering, builder of Stuart trailers, put together this demonstration unit in the late 1940s. It's loaded with 1946–1947 Ford products and pulled by a Ford COE tractor of the same era.

did not reintroduce its diesel models but other diesel trucks began to grow in popularity, especially on the West Coast. Most auto transporters still favored the medium-duty, gasoline-powered tractor produced by the Big Three or International.

Four-car transporters remained the most popular type of transporters in the postwar years. However, the equipment operated on the East Coast usually differed from that operated out west, in that the western units were longer and lighter in weight. The single-tire, tandem-axle trailers of the 1930s were replaced with single-axle, dual-wheel models. The improvements in vacuum and air brake systems made during World War II made the single-axle models as safe to operate as the older tandem-axle trailers.

In an attempt to increase trailer utilization, some carriers experimented with convertible trailers. In addition to hauling automobiles, these units could be converted to haul general freight. It was proposed that these trailers could haul auto parts into the assembly plants and then haul completed autos out. ICC regulations and protests from the drivers' unions usually precluded widespread use of these trailers. However, this would not be the last time they were tried and rejected.

Since the early 1930s, most of the drivers employed by the auto transporters were members of the Teamsters Union. In the late 1940s, they began to make demands for benefits beyond normal wages. The term "health and welfare benefits" began to be tossed about. The average pay rate was between five and nine cents per mile, but there was talk of hourly wages, as well as loading and unloading pay. It would be a few more years, but eventually the Teamsters would get all these benefits and more.

The auto transport companies were not the only ones short of equipment in the postwar years. Their long-time competitors, the railroads, had also converted many of their Auto Loader boxcars to standard boxcars

The NATA held annual roadeos for the top drivers in their members' fleets. Here, in a postwar roadeo, one of Boutell's drivers in a GMC COE is being judged on his driving skills. *Phillip Baumgarten*

during the war. As automobile production increased, they too, found themselves unable to meet the demand. The automobile manufacturers were forced to ship their new vehicles by whatever means was available, rail, haulaway, or driveaway. In some plants, where before the war, shipments were split between carriers based on a percentage of production or a certain number of units, production was shipped by the first available method. The haulaway companies were, for a while, able to compete with the railroads for the longer, over-the-road hauls. By the end of the 1940s, the haulaway companies were delivering 70 to 75 percent of motor vehicle production, and it was common for shipments from Detroit to Texas or even California to go by truckway.

The postwar Chevrolet trucks, like this one operated by Boutell, were similar to the 1941–1942 models. Note the triangular turn signal lights. On the MHS trailer is a load of 1946 Buicks. *Phillip Baumgarten*

Compare the styling of this 1942 GMC to that of the Chevrolets of the same period. Howard Sober, Inc., operated this GMC out of his Buffalo, New York, terminal. Note the total lack of chrome trim on this "blackout model." *Warren Colpo*

As a contract carrier, Arthur did not participate in the NATA Roadeos. However, Arthur was a member of the A.T.A. and participated in its events, as shown here. Note the stands supporting the loading skids. This postwar trailer is an MHS Clipper model 433.

By 1946, Consolidated Convoy had changed its name to Convoy Company. Five-car equipment like this truck and full-trailer came into use in the late 1940s. Note the position of the fuel tank at the extreme rear of the early postwar Ford truck. The transported units are 1946–1948 Fords. *Ackroyd Photography Inc.*

Kenosha Auto Transport's (KAT) fleet was made up largely of Internationals. These postwar "K" models are loaded with 1946 Nash automobiles. The unit in the foreground is an Illinois special, while following is a conventional four-car semitrailer rig. *Whitehead & Kales*

An Eastern Auto Forwarding Company Dodge fueling up with Richfield gasoline. Its load is two, probably three, late 1940s Dodge trucks. These were the days before modern truck stops and paved fuel plazas.

Rocky Mountain Auto Transport built or had built this Dodge-based five-car rig. Note the large front tires, mounted on ten-stud wheels. The autos are 1946-47-48 Chrysler products. *NATA*

A Dodge-powered KAT Illinois special caught on the move. KAT was the major carrier of Nash autos. Note the rare wood-bodied "Ambassador Suburban" immediately behind the cab. *Joseph Wanchura*

The side view of the Rocky Mountain rig shows the trucks long wheelbase and how the autos were "stacked." It's quite possible that this rig was front wheel drive. *NATA*

Chrysler Corporation continued to ship bodies between plants but its transport equipment has evolved since the 1930s. The bodies are now transported vertically, with another carried behind the cab of the COE Dodge truck.

Four big 1947 Cadillacs ready to leave Buffalo on a new Delavan trailer. This rig, with a new Chevrolet tractor, is operated by Howard Sober, Inc. In the summer months, autos would be shipped to Buffalo by Great Lakes freighter via Lake Erie. Numerous carriers had terminals in Buffalo, from which they delivered into areas of the Northeast. *Warren Colpo*

Accidents happen, as seen here in Rockford, Illinois, in September 1947. One of Arthur's new 1948 Advance-Design Chevrolet trucks has tangled with a K-model International. The 1948 Chevrolet truck was completely restyled but the 1948 Chevrolet autos, shown here, retained the prewar styling. Their restyle would come next year.

Following the Rockford accident, the rig was towed back to Janesville and photographed from every angle. The tractor and MHS trailer suffered extensive damage and all the autos were damaged to some extent. Note the upper car has shifted to the right and fallen out of the left track.

This Advance-Design Chevrolet COE is participating in the 1949 NATA Roadeo. The unit is operated by C&J Commercial Driveaway, hauling 1949 Kaisers. Based in Lansing, Michigan, C&J were primarily Oldsmobile carriers.

As a Common Carrier, Convoy's services were available to anyone in its area who needed vehicles transported. Such was the case in November 1947 when this Model T Ford was shipped on one of its three-car rigs. Note the long wheelbase of the Ford tractor. *Ackroyd Photography Inc.*

The Ford, Mercury, and Lincoln were completely restyled for 1949. Mercurys like these were favorites of hot rodders and customizers in the 1950s. This is a W&K trailer and an early (1946–1947) postwar Ford tractor. Associated Transports was a Ford hauler in the Missouri area. *Joseph Wanchura*

The real 1949 DeSotos were introduced in March of that year. Before that, some carryover 1948s were registered as 1949s. These real 1949s were Chrysler's first restyle since before World War II. DeSotos were above Dodge but below Chrysler in the Chrysler Corporation hierarchy and were only available with the flathead six-cylinder engine. This is a "western" four-car setup, operated by Convoy with a 1948 or 1949 Ford F-5 tractor. Note the fuel tanks behind the cab. *Ackroyd Photography Inc.*

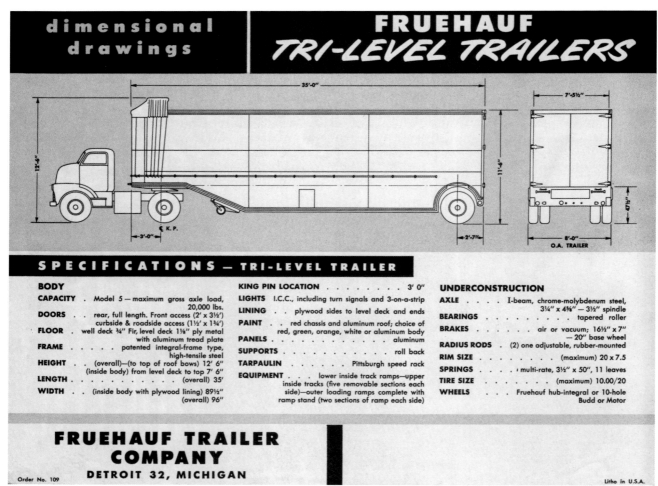

dimensional drawings

FRUEHAUF TRI-LEVEL TRAILERS

SPECIFICATIONS — TRI-LEVEL TRAILER

BODY

CAPACITY . Model 5 — maximum gross axle load, 20,000 lbs.

DOORS . . rear, full length. Front access (2' x 3½') curbside & roadside access (1½' x 1¾')

FLOOR . . . well deck ¾" Fir, level deck 1⅛" ply metal with aluminum tread plate

FRAME . . . . . patented integral-frame type, high-tensile steel

HEIGHT . . (overall)—(to top of roof bows) 12' 6" (inside body) from level deck to top 7' 6"

LENGTH . . . . (overall) 35'

WIDTH . . (inside body with plywood lining) 89½" (overall) 96"

KING PIN LOCATION . . . . 3' 0"

LIGHTS . . I.C.C., including turn signals and 3-on-a-strip

LINING . . plywood sides to level deck and ends

PAINT . . . red chassis and aluminum roof; choice of red, green, orange, white or aluminum body

PANELS . . . . aluminum

SUPPORTS . . . . roll back

TARPAULIN . . . . Pittsburgh speed rack

EQUIPMENT . . . lower inside track ramps—upper inside tracks (five removable sections each side)—outer loading ramps complete with ramp stand (two sections of ramp each side)

UNDERCONSTRUCTION

AXLE . . . . . I-beam, chrome-molybdenum steel, 3¼" x 4⅝" — 3½" spindle

BEARINGS . . . . tapered roller

BRAKES . . . . . . air or vacuum; 16½" x 7" — 20" base wheel

RADIUS RODS . (2) one adjustable, rubber-mounted

RIM SIZE . . . . (maximum) 20 x 7.5

SPRINGS . . . . multi-rate, 3½" x 50", 11 leaves

TIRE SIZE . . . . (maximum) 10.00/20

WHEELS . . . Fruehauf hub-integral or 10-hole Budd or Motor

FRUEHAUF TRAILER COMPANY
DETROIT 32, MICHIGAN

Order No. 109

Litho in U.S.A.

Fruehauf's convertible trailer looked promising in the company's literature but it never found wide acceptance. Convertible trailers would be tried again in the future with much the same results.

CHAPTER 4

The 1950s

The Golden Years

Many of the American soldiers who served in Europe during and after World War II returned home with an interest in the smaller automobiles used there. At the same time, European and British manufacturers were looking for export markets for their products. Every vehicle that they could export to America gave the producing countries U.S. dollars needed to pay war debts. Among the first European vehicles imported in the postwar period was the German Volkswagen. In 1949, only two were officially imported. Two years later, Volkswagen dealers were selling 600 cars each month. Small cars from England, like the Austin and the MG sports car were also popular. France exported its rear-engined Renaults, which for a time, competed favorably with the Volkswagen for sales. By the mid-1950s, nearly every European country was exporting autos to America. Because of their fuel economy and compact size, they became many suburban families' second cars.

The first imports arrived in small numbers and were usually delivered to the dealer or purchaser via driveaway. As the volume of imports increased, the automobile transporters found another source of revenue. On both coasts, transporters with terminals in port cities were in the best position to serve the importers. However, Detroit-based carriers such as Boutell and Sober also became interested in the business as a source of "back hauls." As back haul freight, many of these autos were transported at a reduced rate. It was a win-win situation for the carriers and shippers but it established a precedent that later would be hard to change. The importers began to expect and even demand a rate that was cheaper than that charged the domestic auto makers.

The imported auto's compact size enabled five or more units to be loaded on the four-car rigs, although some trailers had to be modified to accommodate the narrow track of the imports. Some of the new equipment

In 1950, ARCO Auto Carriers and Dealers Transport had common ownership. A joint project of the two companies was the DeARCO auto transporter seen here. It was a five-car unit with the Ford cab mounted high and above the engine and over the nose of the forward auto. The height of this unit restricted its use to areas where there were no low viaducts and underpasses. It was expensive to produce and difficult to operate. *Joseph Wanchura*

GMC introduced its version of Chevrolet's Advance-Design trucks in 1948, and they continued in production with only minor changes through 1953. This COE is delivering a load of 1950 Pontiacs on a MHS M-480 trailer. The opening in the side of the trailer permits access to the driver door of the auto on the bottom front. There is a similar opening on the right rear of the trailer for access to the rear auto. *Phillip Baumgarten*

Operated by E&L Transport, Inc., of Indiana, this 1950 Ford F-6 tractor and Stuart trailer are a matched set. The autos are also 1950 Fords.

built in the mid-1950s was made specifically to haul imports, while other equipment was adaptable to both imports and domestics. As older transport trailers were rebuilt, they were modified to transport import cars more efficiently. In the mid-1950s, Sober had nearly 100 trailers equipped to transport import autos. By 1956, it was transporting for Volkswagen, Jaguar, MG, Mercedes-Benz, Hillman, Porsche, and others, making it the largest transporter of imported autos at that time.

Even with as many as 200,000 autos imported in 1957, the business of transporting these autos was somewhat sporadic. Ships, such as the SS *Ravenstein*, would arrive at a port with as many as 750 autos on board. Upon landing, the autos were towed to a servicing area where gasoline was added and the battery cables were connected. After other fluid levels were checked, they were dispatched to the carriers for final shipment. Within four days, the ship could be unloaded and the vehicles prepped and shipped out. The carriers would then have to wait for another ship to arrive. This was unlike the transporters working out of the domestic assembly plants, where a steady stream of autos came out the door daily. Until the volume of imports

W&K built several of these Dodge-based Skyscrapers for Commercial Carriers in 1950. The COE design enabled five autos to be transported within a 50-foot overall length. This Skyscraper is seen with a load of four 1950 Dodges and a single 1950 Packard. *Phillip Baumgarten*

The 1951 Kaiser was introduced in early 1950. There were no true 1950 Kaiser models, but some 1949s were registered as 1950s. The 1951 was completely restyled by Howard Darrin (Dutch) and carried his famous "Darrin Dip" at the top of the windshield. This 1946 or 1947 Ford, operated by Convoy, is loading two Kaisers. Note that this truck is equipped with sanders. *Ackroyd Photography Inc.*

This is the Convoy four-car rig that was hauling DeSotos in the previous chapter. The upper deck in the middle of the trailer has been dismantled, and it appears that only two Kaisers are going to be loaded this summer day in 1950. Kaiser had an assembly plant in Portland, Oregon, with a capacity of 20 cars a day. Unfortunately, demand for Kaisers fell off and the plant was closed in 1951. *Ackroyd Photography Inc.*

This 35-foot W&K model SCHA trailer had plenty of room for four 1951 Dodges. The tractor is also a Dodge operated by Baker Driveaway, Inc. Baker's rigs were orange with dark blue trim. *Phillip Baumgarten*

increased, few transporters could afford to dedicate a fleet of rigs to transport them exclusively.

American auto makers restyled their autos every two or three years in the 1950s. Each time, they became lower, longer, and sometimes wider. The 1955 models from Chrysler, Ford, and General Motors were all new and some of the largest mass-produced autos ever built. Older transport trailers had to be lengthened and modified to haul the new, larger autos. Sometimes, an extension could be welded to the ends of the decks, providing additional length. However, when preparing for the 1955 models, many trailers had to be cut in half and stretched by welding a new section in between the two halves.

Fortunately, about this same time, many states were beginning to allow longer truck and trailer combinations on their highways. California increased the legal trailer length from 35 to 40 feet in 1953. Pennsylvania extended its maximum combination length to 50 feet in March of 1956. That state also allowed a 30-inch tolerance for auto transport equipment. In most other states, the maximum trailer length was between 35 and 40 feet, with a few states imposing overall length limits, usually 50 to 55 feet.

The eastern transporters had been using the four-car transport trailer since the mid-1930s. As business became more competitive and length laws were relaxed, carriers began to look for ways to add a fifth auto to their loads. The easiest method was to build a rack, called a head rack or head ramp, above the tractor's cab. On short-wheelbase tractors, the vehicle loaded on the head rack extended far to the rear, making modifications to the front of the trailer also necessary. Five-car trailers were also developed in which one or two decks were raised and lowered, either manually or through the use of hydraulics. Kenosha Auto Transport (KAT) built and operated trailers that were adaptable to various types of cargo. By using uprights and decks that were completely removable and adjustable, it could configure its trailers to transport four or five autos or a combination of autos and trucks. These units could also be completely knocked down for use as a flat-bed

Nash introduced its compact Rambler in 1950. Lois Lane used one of the convertibles in the *Superman* television series. Hazel Arthur, owner of ARCO, is seen here dispatching a load of Ramblers on an MHS trailer pulled by a Ford F-6 COE.

Another of Commercial Carriers' Skyscraper rigs with a load of 1951 Dodges. Note the wiper on the lower windshield, which was at the driver's feet. The third axle, with single tires, is a dolly under the trailer's drawbar. *Phillip Baumgarten*

Convoy built 10 of these COE trucks in its own shops. Based on Ford F-8 chassis, they were completely reworked and bore little resemblance to their Dearborn heritage. Like the Skyscraper, these trucks had windows under the windshield. Although Convoy built its own trailers, this one is a Stuart, loaded with 1952 Packards. *Ackroyd Photography Inc.*

trailers. Using this equipment, KAT could haul International or Dodge pickups to the West Coast and return east with large pieces of equipment, such as Elgin street sweepers. The trailers were also adaptable for hauling boats, and KAT became a major transporter of marine equipment in the 1950s.

West Coast carriers had been using five- and six-car equipment for many years. Two of the largest western carriers, Convoy and Western Auto Transports, had their own trailer-building facilities, constructing state-of-the-art equipment. By 1953, Convoy already had seven-car rigs on the highways of Oregon, Washington, and California. Convoy made extensive use of lightweight materials in its trailers, which also featured hydraulically moveable decks. Western shipped autos from Detroit to

Denver or Cheyenne on eastern four-car trailers. For delivery in the West, the autos were transferred to five- or six-car units, some of these driven by two-man driver teams. While one driver drove, the other slept.

Gasoline-powered tractors were still the truck of choice for the eastern transport fleets. However, some carriers employed owner-operators (called brokers), who supplied their own tractors, some of which were diesel powered. Dallas & Mavis Forwarding Company employed a large number of brokers and many of them favored the Mack B-61 diesel. In the West, the diesel was more common, especially for hauling the five- and six-car loads over the Rockies. Convoy purchased a limited number of Ford tilt cabs with diesel engines in 1958, followed by 26 F-800 diesels in 1959.

Hadley has been Ford's principal transporter in the American Southwest since the 1930s. This load of 1952 Mercurys is about to be delivered on a four-car rig with a 1948–1950 Ford tractor.

MOVING CARS WEST

The year 1955 was a boom year for America's automobile producers. Sales of the Big Three's new, larger, and restyled 1955 models skyrocketed. The regional assembly plants scattered across America could not build every make and model and many vehicles had to be shipped to distant points from plants in Detroit and the Midwest.

Western Auto Transports, based in Denver, had the ICC rights to transport autos from various Michigan counties where autos were produced to much of the West. Besides being the delivering carrier for many shipments, it also interchanged or "interlined" with other carriers at points in Iowa, Wyoming, and Utah.

Cadillac and Chrysler were two of Western's primary shippers. Like other carriers, Western was unprepared for the increased number of autos produced and shipped in 1955. Shortly after the new models were introduced, backlogs of unshipped units began to pile up. Chrysler looked

The first leg of the trip west usually began in Michigan. These 1954 Hudsons are about to be loaded on one of Western's W&K four-car trailers. Cab-over tractors, like this Advance-Design Chevrolet, were required on the first two legs of the trip, which traversed Iowa, where length limits were 45 feet. Phillip Baumgarten

to Cassens Transport and other carriers to get their unshipped autos to the dealers. Cassens lacked ICC authority to deliver to the West, so Cassens and Chrysler went before the ICC and asked for a temporary permit. The ICC granted Cassens Transport a 90-day temporary authority to haul autos from Detroit to California, Washington, and Oregon. Hopeful that the authority would become permanent, Cassens purchased 100 new tractors and trailers for use in the operation. However, at the end of the 90-day period, Western was able to prove to the ICC that it could handle the traffic to the West without Cassens' help. It did so by lining up additional brokers and by "trip leasing" with other carriers, such as Howard Sober. Unlike general freight carriers, auto transporters were permitted to lease each other unused equipment for periods as short as a single trip. Hence the term, "trip leasing."

Cadillac's traffic department also attempted to bypass Western's authority in order to get its backlog of unshipped autos west. Cadillac turned to Commercial Carriers, its eastern carrier, and contracted with it to haul the autos west to St. Louis, Missouri. There, Associated Transports, a carrier with authority in St. Louis, picked up the autos and delivered them to Phoenix, Arizona. In Phoenix, the autos were turned over to Robertson Truck-A-Ways, a California carrier, who delivered them to dealers in California. Other autos were interlined with KAT in Salt Lake City for destinations in northern California and Oregon. This interlining or relaying of shipments would have been legal, had it not been done to circumvent Western's authority. Western went before the ICC, protested, and again showed that it could now handle the increased shipment. The ICC ordered Commercial Carriers and the other transporters to cease their interlin-

West of Denver or Cheyenne, Western could legally operate longer combinations with conventional cabs and 35-foot trailers. Photographed outside Western's Denver terminal is a 1956 Dodge V-8, loaded with 1957 Chrysler products. Beside it is an empty 1955 Ford, also V-8 powered. Neil Sherff

Western built much of its own equipment, like this trailer pulled by a Mack tractor. These trailers could be knocked down for use as flat beds. The Mack is a lightweight Western LTL-model. Phillip Baumgarten

West of Denver, Western operated some sleeper-cab trucks with two-man teams. This mid-1950s Kenworth sleeper and full trailer was one of those units. While one driver slept, the other drove. This load of 1956 automobiles consists of a Rambler Cross Country station wagon, an Imperial, and four Plymouth Furys; 1956 was the first year for the Fury, and only 4,485 were built that year. Phillip Baumgarten

These 1957 Ford cars and station wagons are on a 1956 Ford V-8 truck operated by Western. After delivering autos shipped from the Midwest, Western loaded Fords and other autos assembled in California and hauled them back to Denver and Cheyenne. Phillip Baumgarten

This six-car rig is Freightliner-based and uses a semitrailer instead of the full trailer and converter dolly seen on the Kenworth. This load of lumber may be an attempt to back haul something other than automobiles. It appears to have been difficult to load and unload. Then again, it may have been a load of lumber for a Western building project. The early 1950s "bubble-nose" Freightliner was one of the first models of that marque to be sold to operators other than Consolidated Freightways. Phillip Baumgarten

ing operations. To the dealers' consternation, Cadillac responded by shipping half of the West Coast units by railroad boxcar. Besides the additional transport time required by rail, it was almost impossible to get four big Cadillacs in or out of a 40-foot boxcar. When the number of complaints from dealers became great enough, Cadillac's traffic department increased the number of vehicles going west by truckaway.

Hauling autos to the West Coast in the pre-Interstate Highway System days was long and hard, and Western attempted to make the trip easier by relaying their shipments. Autos were loaded in Detroit or Jackson, Michigan, and sent west to Iowa for the first leg of the relay. From Iowa, a new driver, sometimes with a new tractor, would take the load to Denver or Cheyenne. There,

the trailer might be unloaded and the autos sorted for their ultimate destination. The autos would then be loaded on longer West Coast five- or six-car equipment for final delivery. Once in California, these trucks would then be used to transport Fords and other autos built in the West Coast plants back to Denver and Cheyenne.

Long distance truckaway of automobiles was very expensive, even in the 1950s. About the same time that the railroads began to offer piggyback transport, Western's owners were approached by Commercial Carriers with a buyout offer. By 1958, Western was no more, and Commercial was Cadillac's carrier to the West Coast. Commercial continued to haul Cadillacs west until the mid-1960s, when it could no longer compete with the multi-level rail car rates.

However, it continued to buy and use both gasoline and diesel equipment side by side for many years. Western also employed many brokers and their diesel equipment included GMCs, Macks, Peterbilts, Kenworths, and Freightliners.

On both coasts and in between, the auto transporters' fleets always included large numbers of Ford, Dodge, and GM tractors. Normally when a carrier had a contract with one of the major automobile manufacturers, it used that manufacturer's trucks in its fleet. Sober used Chevrolets and GMCs to haul GM products (mostly Oldsmobiles in the 1950s) but Sober's fleet included other makes. Sober was a major transporter for Reo and

International, usually via driveaway, so it had a few Reo and International tractors in use. Sober's Chrysler-hauling operation in Detroit was operated with the use of a large number of brokers, many of whom owned Dodges. Convoy hauled autos for every American manufacturer and most of the importers. It established a policy of purchasing equipment from the different manufacturers based on the percentage of business that manufacturer's products represented as a part of Convoy's business. If, for instance, the vehicles transported for Chrysler represented 10 percent of its total business, Convoy's next truck purchase might include 10 percent Dodges. Companies like

E. P. Hadley proudly endorsed Champion Spark Plugs in this 1953 ad. The equipment and autos pictured date back three years. The five-car sleeper rig is a 1948–1950 Ford.

Robert Walker and George F. Burnett, Inc., who mainly transported Studebakers, operated a large number of Studebaker trucks in fleets. KAT was primarily contracted with Nash (later American Motors Corporation) and could have used any make equipment. However, its fleet was largely made up of Internationals, as it was a major transporter of International's light- and medium-duty trucks.

In the late 1950s, all the medium-duty truck manufacturers offered V-8 engines and they came to be popular with many of the transporters. Air brakes also became almost universally accepted as the safest trailer braking system. In some states like Washington and Oregon, air brakes were required on semitrailers. The heavier five- and six-car loads were simply too much for the vacuum brake-equipped rigs, especially on the long downgrades.

The railroads continued to aggressively solicit auto-hauling business in the 1950s. In 1953, trailer on flatcar (TOFC) shipment of general freight semitrailers, called piggyback, was offered to shippers by the railroads. Tried unsuccessfully in the past, advances in equipment now made loading and unloading simpler. In a very short time, developments were made that enabled two semitrailers to be transported on a special 85-foot railroad flatcar.

The 1951 and 1952 Ford trucks acquired a new grille, as seen on this air brake-equipped 1952 tractor operated by Pontiac Auto Transport, Inc. Despite its name, Pontiac Auto Transport was a Buffalo-based Ford carrier. The autos are 1952 Fords.

An Advance-Design Chevrolet COE with a load of 1953 Buicks. The trailer is a W&K with cutouts in the side panels for access to the auto's doors. Note Boutell's new motto, "Safety Is No Accident." *Neil Sherff*

The 1953 Ford trucks were completely restyled, as seen on this "Custom Cab" unit operated by Eastern Transit, Inc. The 1953 Ford cars on the MHS trailer have undergone a minor face-lift for 1953. *Neil Sherff*

Although there were other makes of trucks in Sober's fleet, GMCs were the most common. Here, mechanics are busy servicing five COE GMCs at the Sober facility in Lansing, Michigan. The first trailer in line (No. 142-A) is an MHS Clipper model 414. *NATA*

To keep up with the increased sales of the 1955 model automobiles, most auto transporters had to purchase additional equipment. Baker Driveaway is test loading this new W&K trailer with a load of 1955 Chryslers. The tractor is one of Baker's mid-1950s Dodges. *Phillip Baumgarten*

Enclosed trailers, like this Stuart, offered total protection for the lower autos. The vehicles on the top deck were exposed to the elements but far enough off the highway to be safe from gravel or stone damage. This early 1950s COE Ford belongs to the trailer's manufacturer, Traffic Transport Engineering.

There are approximately 24 loads of 1955 Dodge autos in this photo, which was staged on a Detroit freeway. The tractors are also Dodges leased to Commercial Carriers. Note the missing grille bars and the holes above the grille opening on the COE in the foreground. This was an attempt to increase the flow of air to the radiator.

Another convoy of 1955 Chrysler products on the freeway in Detroit. Note the third truck is a Chevrolet COE, while the other four are Dodges, as you would expect to see hauling Chrysler autos. Passing these rigs are a 1951 Ford, 1954 Mercury, 1953 and 1954 Chevrolets, and a 1955 Cadillac.

These 1955 Chryslers and Plymouths are on quick loaders operated by several different Detroit releasing companies. The tractors are all Dodges dating from 1949 to 1953. Note the virtual "sea" of unshipped autos parked behind these rigs.

In mid-1955, Dodge adopted a wraparound windshield to its 1955 model trucks. While these two tractors, operated by KAT are 1954s or early 1955s with flat windshields, the pickups are second series models with the new windshield design.

The 1955 Nash was restyled with inboard headlamps. Two 1955s are about to be unloaded from a Southern Pacific Auto Loader boxcar. The Nashes had been in a raised position in the ends of the rail car and the two autos that were transported on the floor have already been removed. *Ackroyd Photography Inc.*

By 1956, the imported auto invasion was heating up. Here's Convoy's Number 124, a shop-built COE, with seven oval-window Volkswagens. *Ackroyd Photography Inc.*

Arthur had this five-car equipment built in 1956. The tractor is a 1956 Chevrolet 5400 Series, while the trailer (lettered Arthur Special) was built by the Fox Manufacturing Company in Janesville, Wisconsin. Chevrolet's trucks were now known as Task Force models. The load consists of five 1956 Chevrolets—two Bel Airs and three Two-Tens.

Driveaway remained the primary method of delivery for medium- and heavy-duty trucks in the 1950s. Some dealers insisted on truckaway and the trailer manufacturers began offering trailers designed to transport bigger trucks. Auto Convoy is the operator of this W&K model SCHL truck-trailer with a load of 1956 Fords. Auto Convoy's tractor is a 1955 Ford COE. *Phillip Baumgarten*

Traffic Transport built trailers to transport even larger trucks, like these 1956 Ford tandems. Note the outside dual wheels have been removed from the truck on the bottom deck to provide clearance. E&L's tractor is a 1954 Ford V-8 COE. *Neil Sherff*

E&L Transport also transported Ford agricultural tractors. Here, in 1957, a load is about to leave the Highland Park plant. The tandem axle Stuart trailer has been specially built for transporting tractors. The truck tractor is a 1955 Ford F-800.

MILITARY VEHICLE MOVEMENTS

During World War II, military vehicles and equipment were the sole source of freight for many auto transporters. In peacetime, that freight supplemented the new car shipments as a source of revenue for many carriers.

In the early 1950s, the federal government began to purchase new military vehicles to replace the World War II vintage equipment still in use. Most of the new vehicles were improved models but still similar to their World War II era predecessors. As the new equipment entered service (sometimes delivered by the auto transporters), the serviceable older vehicles were transferred to reserve or National Guard units. Other equipment that was not considered obsolete was returned to depots for rebuilding before redistribution. While the transporters based near the assembly plants received contracts for delivering new military vehicles, transporters in other areas were allocated much of the redistribution work. Unlike civilian dealers, whose vehicles are shipped by the factories, the government usually buys vehicles and arranges its own shipping. The photos on these pages show military vehicle movements in the 1950s. Note that the equipment is both wartime and postwar vintage.

In 1953, when this photo was taken, the government still had large amounts of World War II equipment. Seven of the eight Jeeps in this load are World War II Willys MB or Ford GPW models. The eighth, the one riding immediately behind the cab, is a postwar M38 model. The M38 came into service in 1950; note its larger headlights. Convoy's transporter is one of their shop-built COEs. Ackroyd Photography Inc.

The M38 Jeep was superseded by a new model, the M38A1, in 1952. The M38A1 had the wider body with rounded fenders and hood later used on the civilian CJ-5. A new F-head four-cylinder engine powered the M38A1. Western Auto Transport's driver is tying-down an M38A1 on one of Western's shop-built trailers. The tractor is a second-series 1955 Dodge. Phillip Baumgarten

The replacement for the World War II Dodge weapons carrier was the Dodge M37, officially known as the "Truck, 3/4-ton, 4x4, cargo, M37." More than 80,000 were built, beginning in 1950 and ending in the late 1960s. This load of four U.S. Air Force M37s is being transported on one of Convoy's 1957 Ford tilt cabs. Note that two wheels and tires have been removed from each of the M37s on the trailer. This was necessary to reduce the overall height. Ackroyd Photography Inc.

The ambulance version of the M37 was the M43, seen here on a Convoy truck and semitrailer combination. Convoy's truck pulling this load is a 1953 Ford F-600. Previously, Ford trucks were rated F-1, F-2, etc. In 1953, Ford began using the F-100, F-200, etc., ratings that continue today. Ackroyd Photography Inc.

These World War II bomb carriers were built by Ford Motor Company and remained in service with the U.S. Navy throughout the 1950s. They towed bomb trailers and were used for loading and unloading bombs. Note the long wheelbase of the Western's sleeper-equipped GMC COE. Phillip Baumgarten

These are the bomb trailers that were towed in gangs behind the bomb carriers. Note the winter equipment on the big F-8 Ford from 1949 or 1950, sanders in front of the rear wheels, and tire chains stowed on the spare tire. Ackroyd Photography Inc.

The armed forces purchased large numbers of civilian vehicles for administrative use. This five-car rig, consisting of a 1948 Ford F-7 and a full trailer, is transporting five 1953 Dodge pickups for the Air Force. Here's another case in which the wheels and tires have been removed from the rear axle of the pickup over the cab. Just a few inches of clearance make the difference. Ackroyd Photography Inc.

This International L model is another civilian vehicle in U.S. Air Force service. Western is performing this delivery, using a Dodge COE from the 1951–1953 era. Although the grille bars have been removed, possibly for additional cooling, there is also a "winter front" in rolled-up position above the grille. Also note the "No Riders" sign in the windshield. Phillip Baumgarten

Convoy is using a 1940s Kenworth COE to transport this load of Air Force equipment. The small trailer is a 1/4-ton Jeep trailer. The trucks are 2 1/2 -ton, 6x6, cargo trucks, M35. These were the replacement for the wartime GMC "deuce and a half" trucks, which were similar. Reo Motors built the first M35s, and a single-tire model, the M34, was also built in limited numbers. These Air Force M35s are fitted with the optional hardtop cab. Ackroyd Photography Inc.

GMC also built a version of the postwar "deuce and a half." Its design was also built in single-tire (M135) and dual-wheel (M211) models. A unique feature of the GMC was its automatic transmission. These U.S. Army M135s have had their canvas cab and bed covers removed for truck shipment. Western's tractor is an early 1950s Peterbilt diesel. Phillip Baumgarten

This is a combination shipment of M37s and M35s on Convoy's F-8 Fords. Normally, these military trucks were seen with canvas cab covers. However, again, the Air Force units are equipped with hardtop cabs. Ackroyd Photography Inc.

This 37,500-pound Mack LR dump truck is a full load for one of Convoy's F-8 Fords. The Mack is an Air Force unit, powered by a Cummins NHB600 diesel engine. Ackroyd Photography Inc.

A 1955 Ford Mainline coming off Wright Way's six-car rig. The Mainline was the cheapest Ford model for 1955, devoid of chrome and sometimes used by police agencies. *Ackroyd Photography Inc.*

Wright Way Transport was Alaska's best-known auto transporter. Its equipment, like this 1955 Ford Big Job, was similar to that used by Convoy in the Northwest. *Ackroyd Photography Inc.*

After being completely restyled in 1955, the 1956 Chryslers received a face-lift and modest tail fins. One of Automobile Shippers' Dual Motors trailers is loaded and ready to move out with four 1956 Chryslers. The COE Dodge tractor dates from the early 1950s and is missing some grille bars.

Renault and Simca were the most popular French autos imported in the 1950s. Five Simca Arondes and two Vedettes have been loaded on a Western rig specially constructed to transport smaller, import autos. The tractor is a B-series Mack. *Phillip Baumgarten*

Dodge offered completely restyled autos for 1957. Its trucks, however, received only new front end sheet metal. Cassens operated this 1957 tractor with a new MHS trailer, hauling 1957 Dodge station wagons, which Chrysler called Suburbans.

In 1957, Convoy added some of the East Coast type of Troyler trailers to its fleet. It's possible that Convoy intended to use these trailers in piggyback service, as their West Coast units were not suited for that purpose. Note the extremely short wheelbase on this 1957 Dodge tractor. *Ackroyd Photography Inc.*

GMCs of the 1955–1957 period were similar to their Chevrolet brothers but with more exotic grille work. This COE operated by Dixie Auto Transport Company of Jacksonville, Florida, is loaded with four 1957 Cadillacs. *Neil Sherff*

Ford introduced this tilt cab C-model in 1957. Convoy immediately put a few in its fleet, like this six-car rig transporting five 1957 Cadillacs. *Ackroyd Photography Inc.*

Convoy called this type of equipment "truckyback." The uprights and decks on these C-model Fords could be disassembled and two rigs could be loaded, one on the other, for the return trip when there was no back haul. *Ackroyd Photography Inc.*

The standard grille on the 1955–1957 Chevrolet and GMC trucks was also somewhat garish. Some fleet operators, like Anchor Motor Freight, were more interested in economy than styling. For that reason GM offered a "fleet-option grille" that was the simple wire mesh affair seen here. The COE models of this period were known as LCFs. Anchor's Fruehauf trailer is loaded with 1957 Chevrolets. *Harry Patterson*

Ford introduced the retractable hardtop Skyliner in 1957. Three of them are seen here, along with a Country Squire, which was Ford's premium station wagon. They made for a heavy and expensive load for E&L Transport's 1956 Ford COE and Stuart trailer.

Eastern transporters, like Nu Car Carriers, also used the new Ford tilt cab. This is another load of 1957 Fords on a W&K trailer. *Harry Patterson*

Chrysler's tank plant in Newark, Delaware, was converted to automobile production in the mid-1950s. Metropolitan Convoy Corporation was one of several carriers serving the Newark plant in 1957. Two Forward Look 1957 Plymouths have been loaded on this Delavan trailer, pulled by a 1957 Dodge D-500 tractor.

This 1953 GMC with sleeper box was operated by Convoy in 1957. In the background a trailer load of 1957 Cadillacs is about to be unloaded. The canvas curtains protect the expensive autos in transit. *Ackroyd Photography Inc.*

Ford trucks received a major restyle for 1957. This F-800, probably operated by a broker leased to Automobile Transport, Inc., is Custom Cab-equipped with chrome grille and windshield molding. Four 1957 Lincolns are a tight fit on the Stuart trailer. *Neil Sherff*

Carriers with Studebaker contracts usually had some Studebaker trucks in their fleets. George F. Burnett Company operated many Studebakers like this 1956 V-8 loaded with 1957 Studebaker autos. The trailer is an MHS. *Neil Sherff*

Robert R. Walker, Inc., was another Studebaker carrier. Studebaker-Packard Corp. used this photo of one of its rigs in their 1957 truck brochure. Note the Studebaker Hawk cars on the trailer.

Vauxhalls were built by GM's British subsidiary and sold here by selected Pontiac dealers. Insured Transporters, a California carrier, was transporting these Vauxhalls in the American Southwest on this tired looking 1951 Ford truck and shop-built trailer. Information supplied with this photo indicates that the truck was powered by a Chrysler Hemi motor. Possibly it was running a little hot this day. *James Rowe*

The 1958 Ford cars received a new grille, taillights, and side trim. Four 1958s are seen here on a lightweight "Troyler" transport trailer. Although the 1956 Ford tractor present in this photo is not equipped with one, this trailer was designed to be used with a head rack-equipped tractor. Auto Convoy is the operator of this rig.

This dirty 1957 Ford tilt cab is loaded with 1959 Ford products. Automotive Conveying was Ford's carrier out of the Metuchen, New Jersey, assembly plant. Note the number of license plates of varying sizes. *Harry Patterson*

Five 1959 Buicks must have been a heavy load for this GMC COE and W&K trailer. Note how far the car on the head rack extends to the rear of the tractor. Automobile Carriers worked out of Flint, Michigan. *Neil Sherff*

Albert Cassens endorsed Bendix-Westinghouse air brakes in this 1957 advertisement. Their rig, a 1956 Dodge and a W&K trailer, is loaded with 1957 Chryslers. Note the large size of the 1957 autos, Imperials on top and Chryslers on the bottom.

Orange and red was Boutell's color scheme in the 1950s and beyond. This 1957 Chevrolet LCF is loaded with 1959 Buicks. Note there are only two cab-top marker lights on this tractor. *Neil Sherff*

Anchor Motor Freight was a contract carrier serving much of the Northeast. It is also using a W&K five-car rig, but with a 1958 Chevrolet conventional cab tractor. Note the 1959 Impala convertible in the bottom of the trailer, behind the cab. On the rear is a Chevrolet panel truck. These were the days before minivans. *Neil Sherff*

Fender mirrors, West Coast mirrors, and fog lights dress up this 1959 Chevrolet Viking. The lack of a "V" under the bow tie hood emblem identifies the tractor as a six-cylinder model. The 1959 Pontiacs are riding on a W&K trailer that has been lengthened and has extensions welded to the forward top deck. *Neil Sherff*

An ocean of Ramblers at American Motors Corporation's shipping yard in Kenosha, Wisconsin. Note the variety of AMC cars, the standard size Rambler, compact American and, in the bottom of the trailer in the foreground, a top-of-the-line Ambassador.

This broker, leased to Automobile Transport, Inc., is operating a Mack B-model. It should have had plenty of power to pull the Stuart trailer loaded with 1958 Lincoln and Mercury autos. Note the big M in the grille of the Mercury. Mercury's 1957 advertising referred to the car as the "Big M." *Neil Sherff*

The Edsel was the sensation of the auto industry in 1958. Two and one-half years later, the Edsel name was dead. Nu Car Carriers is using a 1956 Ford F-750 Big Job and Troyler trailer to deliver four 1958 Edsels. *Harry Patterson*

After a complete restyle in 1957, Chrysler's automobiles were only face-lifted for 1958. Quad headlights, which were optional in 1957, were now standard equipment. "Auto Pilot" was Chrysler's trade name for cruise control. This Dodge tractor, a 1958 V-8, is leased to Automobile Shippers, Inc.

The 1959 Chevrolet trucks were similar to the 1958s. The V under the bow tie identifies this 1959 as a V-8. Three Ramblers and an American have been loaded on a Stuart trailer. *Neil Sherff*

Here's a good view of the fleet option grille that GMC offered to truck operators who didn't care about the ornate standard grille. Motorcar Transport was a dedicated Pontiac carrier, as the sign on the grille proclaims. The tractor is a 1957 GMC, with a W&K trailer and 1959 Pontiac autos. *Neil Sherff*

The 1958 and 1959 Dodge COE models retained the 1957 front end styling, with single headlights. This 700 series V-8, leased to Commercial Carriers, is a 1959, identifiable by the bulges on the cowl, hood side, and door.

In the 1950s, the trip to Alaska via the Al-Can Highway was no Sunday afternoon ride. Much of the highway was still gravel surfaced. The autos on this "narrow nose" Kenworth and West Coast type trailer have had their windshields covered for protection from flying gravel. Above the cab is a 1958 Ford, while behind is a 1955 Oldsmobile and an early 1950s Packard. *Joseph Wanchura*

Short-hood GMC DR diesel models, like this one with a sleeper box, were rarely used by auto transporters. This one is leased to KAT and is pulling one of KAT's convertible trailers, rigged to transport five Ramblers in addition to the one over the cab. Two more Ramblers can be seen in the background on another KAT rig. *Neil Sherff*

The 1959 Chevrolet autos featured horizontal tail fins that triggered rumors of the cars becoming "light" in the rear end at high speeds. Their styling, like all of GM's cars that year, was all new. Two loads of 1959s are ready to roll on Fruehauf trailers operated by Complete Auto Transit. The tractor is a 1959 Chevrolet LCF. *Neil Sherff*

Contract Cartage with a load of 1959 Wide Track Pontiacs, three Bonnevilles, and a Catalina. Contract's GMC COE has the standard GMC grille and is pulling a Troyler trailer. *Neil Sherff*

As various states relaxed their length laws, longer equipment came into use. This is a company-owned 1959 Dodge D-700 with the 354-cid hemi V-8. Automobile Shippers, Inc., was owned by Eugene Cassarol, who also built the Chrysler-based sports car, the Dual Ghia. His trailer and automobile building subsidiary, Dual Motors, built the trailer and head rack.

Rear view of the Automobile Shippers five-car rig, with loading almost completed. The 1959 Dodges were big cars. Note how the units on the top deck overlap.

Trailer on flatcar, or piggyback as it was better known, began to catch on in the late 1950s. Some of the earliest destination railheads were in Oklahoma and Texas, areas served by the Auto Convoy Company. In this photo, one of Auto Convoy's 1959 Dodge tractors is unloading a four-car trailer load of 1959 Chrysler products from the flatcar in the background.

Volvo got its toehold in the United States market by selling these PV544 models that resembled scaled down 1948 Fords. Their exceptional performance and durability helped establish the Swedish auto's reputation as solid cars. Boutell has welded an extension to the top deck of this Delavan trailer to accommodate an additional small car in each load. The tractor is a 1958 GMC. *Neil Sherff*

The Ford tilt cab received quad headlights in 1958. Automobile Transport, Inc., is transporting 1959 Lincolns and Mercury station wagons on this old reworked MHS trailer. *Neil Sherff*

We'll have to take Convoy's word that these are 1959 Thunderbirds. More than mere protection from tree limb scratches, these are full car covers, protecting the entire vehicle. Since this photo was taken in the summer of 1959, when the 1959s had already been on sale for almost a year, the covers can't be for purpose of concealing the styling. A 1959 Ford Big Job is doing the job of toting the six personal luxury cars. *Ackroyd Photography Inc.*

The Rambler American, an early compact auto, was introduced in 1959. However, it wasn't really new. Nash began building the compact 100-inch wheelbase Nash Rambler in 1950. In the mid-1950s, Rambler became a separate make, the body was squared off, and the wheelbase grew to 108 inches. For the 1959 model year, Rambler reintroduced the old 100-inch car with a new grille and trim. With a full year's jump on the compacts from the Big Three, it sold very well. Here, in 1959, KAT has succeeded in building a six-car load on five-car equipment. The trailer is one of KAT's convertible models and the tractor is an International West Coaster diesel. *Neil Sherff*

The 1960s

Diesels on the Interstate

Detroit had been watching the growth of the imported automobile market throughout the 1950s. American Motors Corporation also caught Detroit's attention with its very successful compact, the Rambler. As the Big Three's sales plummeted in the 1958 recession, Rambler's sales actually increased. Chrysler, Ford, and GM met the imports and Rambler head-on in the 1960 model year with their own compact automobiles, the Valiant, Falcon, and Corvair. Two years later, they introduced midsize autos like the Ford Fairlane and Chevy II. By the middle of the decade, every major U.S. auto manufacturer offered three or more different size automobiles: compact, midsize, full-size, or sporty cars. The smaller automobiles allowed the auto transporters to increase the number of autos transported in a load without increasing the size of their equipment. With minor modifications, a five-car transporter could haul six compacts. On the West Coast, eight- and nine-car loads were possible.

Similarly, the popularity of the Volkswagen microbus and van led GM, Ford, and later Chrysler, to introduce compact vans and wagons based on their small car components. The introduction of the International Scout and Ford Bronco, along with increased popularity of the civilian Jeep, also provided the auto transporters with a variety of vehicles to transport. The transporters began to look for equipment that was convertible or adaptable to vehicles of different sizes and shapes.

Hydraulically operated, moveable trailer decks had been in limited use since the mid-1950s. Transport companies and trailer manufacturers worked together to develop trailers capable of transporting more automobiles of varying types. In 1960, the five-car rig was still the most common piece of equipment used on the East Coast, where many states still enforced 45-foot overall length limits. When the length limits were increased to 50 feet in 1963, six-car rigs were possible. Seven-car equipment began to appear in 1965, coinciding

Convoy's deliveries to more distant dealers were made on higher-capacity equipment, like this seven-car 1960 Dodge truck and trailer. Four 1960 Valiants, two full-size Plymouths, and a DeSoto are in this load.
Ackroyd Photography Inc.

By 1960, Convoy was able to transport eight Ford Falcons on its lightweight equipment. This was the Falcon's first year. Note the assortment of license plates on this 1957 Ford F-800 Big Job. *Ackroyd Photography Inc.*

with 55-foot overall limits. In areas where length limits were not as restrictive, especially in the Far West, larger, higher-capacity rigs were in operation. In order to get these higher-capacity loads the automobiles had to be loaded differently than in the past, sometimes to within very close tolerances. The autos were driven or backed onto decks that were then raised or lowered hydraulically into traveling position.

The loaded weight of the higher-capacity trailers required that they be equipped with tandem axles. The first trailers used conventional steel spring suspensions, but in the mid-1960s, several carriers began to experiment with air suspension systems. They quickly became the suspension system of choice for many transporters because of the improved ride and handling, especially when the trailer was empty. Today, most auto transport trailers are equipped with air suspension systems.

In states where trucks were weighed and the weight on each axle or sets of axles was calculated, the increased weight of the larger transport trailers often caused the two-axle tractors to be overloaded. This was

Like the Volkswagen, Chevrolet's Corvair was rear engined and air cooled. As the Corvair's popularity increased, it became available in additional body styles and trim levels. These 1961 Corvairs have been loaded on a W&K trailer specially constructed for compact autos. This trailer employed one pair of hydraulic lifts, on the deck immediately behind the cab. The auto on this deck was backed on, with the deck in an inclined position. It was then raised into a horizontal position for traveling, and another auto was driven in, partly under the raised auto.

ANCHOR MOTOR FREIGHT'S DIESELS AND ANCHOR'S CLANKERS

Anchor Motor Freight was one of America's largest auto transporters in the 1960s. Like Arthur in Wisconsin, Anchor began in the 1930s as a contract carrier for Chevrolet, serving plants and dealers in the Northeast. In the 1960s, it operated more than 1,500 tractor and trailer combinations hauling Chevrolets and other GM products out of seven assembly plants and five railheads.

Because of its relationship with GM, Anchor's fleet always consisted of Chevrolet and GMC tractors. In

1963, Anchor purchased two diesel-powered tractors for use as pilot models. Although they were more expensive to purchase than gasoline equipment, the diesel's fuel economy was more than 2 miles per gallon better than the gasoline tractor's 4 miles per gallon. Diesel fuel actually cost less than gasoline in the 1960s, so the fuel savings were even greater. When the pilot vehicles reached 50,000 miles, Anchor had accumulated enough data to justify additional diesel purchases. By mid-1967, Anchor

Anchor's first diesels, in 1963, were installed in heavy-duty GM tractors like these Chevrolets. Single-axle tractors and trailers were the norm with six-car equipment. These 1965 Buicks are riding on equipment based in Wilmington, Delaware. Harry Patterson

By the late 1970s, Anchor standardized on GM's short-hood conventionals like this GMC 9500. Although seen here with a single-axle five-car trailer, the pusher axle indicates that this tractor could also be used in seven-car combinations. Note the single tire on the pusher axle. The cars are 1971 Buicks. Joseph Wanchura

This Chevrolet 90-series was based in Lordstown, Ohio, and hauled Chevrolet Vegas on a Bankhead trailer. Note that by the early 1970s, even the head rack was equipped with a pair of hydraulic lift cylinders. Again, note the missing tire on the pusher axle. Harry Patterson

This Anchor rig, with a load of Oldsmobile Cutlass models, is beginning to look a little worn. Possibly it's one that Overdrive *referred to in its story. Note the front fenders which have been cropped to allow the tilting hood to clear the head rack. These Bankhead trailers were air suspended.* Russell MacNeil

had 300 diesels on the road and an additional 300 on order. Two different diesels were initially tried, both GM Detroits. On their seven-car rigs, Anchor used the 6V-53N, a V-6, while the six-car transporters used the in-line 6-71NE. Anchor expected to increase tractor life cycles from four years to six years, and, in fact, many of its diesel tractors were in use even longer than that. In the 1980s, it was common to see 12- or 15-year-old diesel tractors still hauling autos.

By the end of the 1960s, all of Anchor's new tractor purchases were diesel. Because of Anchor's favorable experience with diesels, its parent company, Leaseway Transportation, began putting diesels in other fleets in the Leaseway system.

In 1967, a fleet management publication praised Anchor's high standards of maintenance and its progressive thinking regarding diesel power and air suspensions. Ten years later, another trucking magazine, *Overdrive*, would charge that Anchor's rigs were some of the worst junk on the highway. *Overdrive* originally published an article claiming that the large LTL fleets like Yellow Freight operated equipment that was unsafe. The magazine's view was, that while the federal and state governments inspected and "deadlined" owner-operators for equipment deficiencies, they turned a blind eye to the shoddy equipment operated by regulated carriers. As a result of the article, *Overdrive* claimed to have received letters from drivers for Anchor who stated that their equipment was worse than that described in the original article. *Overdrive* sent reporters out into the field, and they did indeed find Anchor rigs with numerous defects and extremely shoddy

Ever wonder what happens to old car haulers? Some are cut up for scrap; others are sold and are used by independents, while others go on to other vocations. This old (1970s) ex-Anchor Chevrolet 90 went on to become a dump truck. The cropped fenders remain, as does the front bumper, once part of the head rack.

repair work. In a follow-up article, this was reported, and the rigs were dubbed "Anchor's Clankers." It's doubtful that the rigs the reporters found represented the condition of the entire Anchor fleet. However, few transporters were able to purchase new equipment at that time because of the uncertain state of the domestic automobile industry. In the late 1970s, Anchor purchased many new Brigadiers and Bruins to replace some of its clankers. The new vehicles usually went into service on the longer hauls out of the assembly plants, while the older rigs were used for local deliveries and at the railheads.

More compacts appeared in 1961. Among them were these 1961 Buick Specials, riding on a new GMC 5000 V-6 tractor and W&K trailer. This rig could also transport six standard-size cars. *Neil Sherff*

Full covers on these Ramblers may be to disguise the new styling on the 1961 American. Note this B-model Mack, leased to KAT, has an integral sleeper. *Neil Sherff*

especially true when an additional car was transported on a head ramp. Most eastern carriers overcame this problem by adding a nonpowered third axle, sometimes called a "tag axle" or "pusher." This axle was usually mounted in front of the driven rear axle and could sometimes be raised when not required. Some carriers, like Anchor Motor Freight and M&G Convoy, used tag axles fitted with single tires. It was common to see these rigs with the outside dual tire removed from the tag axle. Only a small amount of weight rested on these axles and these carriers found that a single tire was sufficient and in compliance with the laws of most states.

In the West, three-axle trucks, many dual drive, had already been in use since the mid-1950s. In the 1960s, the two- or three-axle truck and two-axle semitrailer predominated west of the Rockies. These truck and trailer combinations were distant relatives of the "Illinois specials" of the 1930s and 1940s. As legal limits on length increased and equipment grew larger, the truck and trailer combinations moved farther east. Unlike eastern transporters which had thier fifth wheel mounted on the tractor chassis, behind the cab, these western rigs had their fifth wheel mounted low, at the rear of the chassis. They became known as "stingers." Part of the load, usually two or three autos, was carried on the truck, while the balance rode on the trailer. Most states west of the Mississippi permitted 60- to 65-foot-long stingers with up to a 5-foot overhang. The stinger would not become popular in areas of the East until the 1980s, after deregulation and imposition of federal length limits. Today, the stinger is the most common type of equipment in use.

The use of two trailers, called doubles, for transporting autos has never developed to the extent it has for transporting general freight. In the late 1960s, Convoy Company built 105-foot-long double trailer combinations, which it used to a limited extent in Washington and Oregon. In the East, carriers operating in Ohio and New York State were able to use turnpike doubles on the toll roads of those states. Turnpike doubles were two full-length trailers pulled by a single tractor and operated in combination only on the toll road. Upon exiting the toll road, the rigs were driven into a plaza area, where the double combination was broken down into two single loads. With the introduction of larger stinger equipment in the 1980s, most carriers who had employed turnpike doubles turned to 65- and 75-foot stingers to move the larger shipments across these states.

As more sections of the Interstate Highway System were completed, trucks were able to maintain higher highway speeds and reduce transit times. In most cases, deliveries within 500 miles of the assembly plants were made via truckaway. The higher speeds and heavier

loads required even more powerful tractors than the V-8 rigs of the late 1950s. In 1960, Dodge reentered the diesel truck market with a short-hood model later known as the C model or the LCF. Ford, Chevrolet, and even Studebaker began selling diesel-powered tractors soon after. Many auto transport companies purchased a few of these low-cost diesels as test tractors. Usually, they proved more durable and cheaper to operate than

Volkswagen was the best-selling import in the United States in the 1960s. In addition to the popular Beetle, a sporty Karmann Ghia coupe was also available. This nine-car load on a Convoy 1960 Dodge D-700 includes one Karmann Ghia, the coupe behind the cab. *Ackroyd Photography Inc.*

Of the luxury imports, Mercedes-Benz was the best seller in the 1950s and 1960s. These 1963 Mercedes-Benz autos look very much like their present day counterparts. Note one big coupe on the rear of the trailer. The truck is a 1963 Ford F-850 Super-Duty. *Ackroyd Photography Inc.*

In response to the popularity of the Ford tilt cab, GMC and Chevrolet introduced similar models in 1960. This GMC 5500 V-6 was almost new when this photo was taken in 1960. *Neil Sherff*

Based in Columbus, Ohio, Chrysler Distributor George Byers and Sons operated a fleet of transporters. This GMC tilt cab is loaded with 1962 Valiants and Chryslers. The Valiant on the rear of the semienclosed trailer is a Signet two-door hardtop. *Neil Sherff*

From the mid-1970s on, the most common police cars were four-door sedans. However, in the 1950s and 1960s, two-door police cars were the norm in many areas. There are 29 Plymouth Savoy two-door sedans with police car equipment loaded on these six trailers going to the Michigan State Police. Square Deal Cartage is the carrier, and the lead truck is a 1960 Dodge D-700.

the gasoline models. However, the higher initial cost caused many carriers to continue to buy gasoline-engined tractors for local deliveries. Gasoline and diesel rigs could be found working side by side in many fleets until well into the 1970s.

Piggyback accounted for a large portion of railroad shipments in the early 1960s. In most cases, the railroads transported four-car trailers belonging to the auto transport companies. However, a few railroads owned or leased trailers. The Southern Pacific Railroad even had its own truckaway division, Pacific Motor Trucking (PMT). PMT not only delivered vehicles from the railheads to the dealers, but in the mid-1950s PMT obtained common carrier authority to deliver autos via truckaway out of West Coast assembly plants to all points served by the Southern Pacific Railroad. The New York Central Railroad used a variation of piggyback called "Flexivan." They were transport trailers with removable axles similar to intermodal freight containers. Each Flexivan carried four automobiles and was slid on and off the railroad flatcar. The front of the unit connected to a semitractor fifth wheel, while the rear rode on a set of removable axles.

The piggyback operations required large numbers of "eastern" style four-car trailers. Western-type trailers with their low-mounted king pins were not suitable for use in piggyback operations because they were not compatible with the fifth wheel hook-up used on standard highway and eastern transport tractors. Since the majority of Convoy's equipment was of the stinger variety, Convoy sent representatives out across the country looking for unused eastern-type trailers. At its peak,

The light- and medium-duty Dodge trucks for 1960 received a new grille and little more. Dodge's big news was in its full-size range. This B-model Mack is loaded with five 1960 Dodge Sweptside pickups. The Stuart trailer is equipped with one set of hydraulic lifts operating the forward top deck. *Neil Sherff*

Convoy had about 60 trailers in piggyback service. However, unlike other operators, Convoy unloaded the eastern four-car trailers at the destination railhead and reloaded the automobiles on its higher-capacity equipment for dealer delivery.

The use of bilevel auto rack rail cars developed in the 1950s began to surpass piggyback as the preferred method of rail transport in the 1960s. The multilevel rail cars were quickly loaded and unloaded by a simple drive-on, drive-off method. They enabled the railroads to move greater volumes of vehicles in less time than piggyback. At the same time, the railroads began using trilevel cars capable of transporting up to 18 automobiles each. Because of their greater height, trilevels were restricted from operating in certain areas, but the 12-car bilevels could operate anywhere there were unloading facilities. In the late 1960s, there were about 50 railheads throughout the country. As the multilevel cars became available in volume, piggyback transport decreased and many carriers found themselves with a surplus of obsolete four-car trailers. In 1966, KAT ran an advertisement in *Automotive News* offering to sell 851 convertible four-car trailers that had previously been in use in piggyback operations.

The multilevel rail operations still required the services of the truckaway companies to deliver the new vehicles from the railhead to the dealers. In many cases, they also transported vehicles from the assembly plants to the outbound rail yard. This business has continued to grow, and today more than half of Detroit's new autos are delivered on multilevel rail equipment. The railroads give the multilevel rail cars a higher priority in transit than the old automobile boxcars. Rail transport still is not as fast as truck direct movements, but the financial savings offset the longer delivery time.

Dodge's big news for 1960 was its LCF models, available in diesel and gasoline versions. These short-hood tractors had an 89-inch bumper to back of cab measurement and swing-out fenders for easy service. This early LCF is a model NC-800 operated by Hulbert Forwarding Company of Buffalo. The reworked MHS trailer is loaded with four 1960 Plymouths, while the unit above the cab is a 1960 Dodge Polara.

Enclosed trailers were used for transporting special units and show cars. Because of length laws, it was difficult to operate long trailers with short conventional tractors and still have room for a sleeper box. Commercial Carriers got around that problem by installing a "penthouse" sleeper above the cab of this Dodge LCF. Note the oil filter mounted on the left-side cowl. An external air cleaner is similarly mounted on the right side.

The 1960 Cadillac was a big car, but the Troyler Company figured out how to get five of them on its lightweight 60T112 trailer. The trailer's length was 37 1/2 feet, and with a COE like this GMC tilt cab, the overall length was less than 50 feet. No hydraulics were used on this unit. The decks were positioned manually and their movement was assisted by springs.

This is an earlier model Troyler trailer used by Cassens Transport to transport four 1960 Chryslers. Note how far the bottom car sticks out of the front of the trailer. The 1957 Dodge V-8 tractor appears to be taking a breather. *Neil Sherff*

Although larger equipment was beginning to appear, the four-car rigs were still the most common equipment used east of the Mississippi. E&L is using a late 1950s Ford F-series tractor with a Stuart trailer to haul a 1960 Mercury wagon and three Fords. Note the fastback Starliner on the bottom deck. *Phillip Baumgarten*

Another E&L combination, but this one has a Stuart trailer designed to transport cars, trucks, or a combination of both. The outside tires have been removed from the dual wheels of the medium-duty truck being transported, and they are strapped to the chassis, behind the cab. *Phillip Baumgarten*

The Ford tilt cab was given quad headlights for 1958, 1959, and 1960. They then reverted to single headlamps for the balance of their production run, almost 30 more years. This Super-Duty, operated by Hadley, is equipped with aluminum wheels and Custom Cab trim. The autos are 1960 Fords. *James Rowe*

These 1960 Thunderbirds and Lincolns are on a Stuart trailer and 1959 Ford tractor leased to E&L Transport. Note the sleeper box, rare on eastern equipment at this time. *Neil Sherff*

Another unusual sight is a load of 1960 Chevrolets on a Hadley rig. Hadley was a Ford transporter in California and the Southwest. The tractor is a 1955 Ford V-8. *James Rowe*

Before merging with Diamond T in 1967, Reo and Diamond T shared some models. This Reo B-703D of the early 1960s is very similar to the Diamond T of the same period. This is an owner-operator, leased to KAT. *Neil Sherff*

This photo taken in Detroit shows 1960 Chrysler products of every variety ready to ship. The transporters are all Dodges. The tractor on the left and the fourth from the left are 1958s, as is the COE. The third truck from the left, operated by Dixie Auto Transport of Jacksonville, Florida, is a 1954 or early 1955. At the far end, with a 1960 Valiant on the head rack, is a second series 1955 or 1956.

The Volvo has become very popular with the large auto transport fleets in recent years. However, in 1960, a Volvo truck was a rare sight. This must be one of the first Volvo trucks imported into the United States. It's leased to Case Driveway and the Delavan trailer is loaded with Jeep vehicles. Note two different CJ-models were offered at this time. The two Jeeps without tops are CJ-3B-models with flat fenders. A CJ-5 with rounded fenders and optional hardtop is riding on the rear of the trailer. *Neil Sherff*

Station wagons grew in popularity in the 1950s and 1960s. Most manufacturers offered wagons in two or three trim levels. There are four wagons in this load of five 1960 Chevrolets. Complete Auto Transit's tractor is also a 1960 Chevrolet. *Neil Sherff*

Another rare vehicle is this 1960 Studebaker Transtar, operated by ARCO. Note the trailer has the top deck extended forward about five feet. The bottom deck has also been extended, and the kingpin has been repositioned forward so that the rear tires of the tractor no longer fill the cutouts in the trailer. *Neil Sherff*

The 1961 Fords received new sheet metal, although the rooflines remained the same. Along with three Custom two-doors, there are two Galaxies in this load. The car above the cab has the formal roofline, while the Galaxie in the bottom of the trailer is a Starliner. E&L's tractor is a 1959 Ford. *Phillip Baumgarten*

Dodge pickups were restyled for 1961, but it appears that the designer in charge of the grille took a year off. The simple "chicken wire" design looks unfinished. This B-model Mack with an aftermarket sleeper box is leased to Dallas & Mavis. *Neil Sherff*

The Super-Duty Ford received new, tougher looking styling for 1961. Their 102-inch bumper to back of cab dimension made them popular with auto transporters. This new F-800 is operated by Nu Car Carriers. The four-car trailer is equipped with one set of hydraulic cylinders, operating the top front deck. *Ronald Adams*

Limited access highways, such as the New York State Thruway, permitted the use of double trailers long before other state highways. Commercial Carriers transported 11 1961 Chrysler autos on this double combination. These rigs would be broken down to single units for operation off the Thruway. The tractor is a Dodge diesel CN-800. *Neil Sherff*

Dodge's panel truck and suburban-like Town Wagon were not restyled with the other light-duty Dodge models in 1961. They would retain their 1958 sheet metal through 1964. Three 1961 Town Wagons are seen here on a Stuart transport trailer, pulled by a 1961 Dodge D-700.

Commercial Carriers hauled Cadillacs from Detroit to areas of the West Coast. This Troyler has had a canvas panel added to the lower sides to protect the car riding "in the hole." Note the sleeper on the GMC tilt cab. These are 1961 autos. *Neil Sherff*

Truckers called GMC's big DR-model D the "cracker box" because of its square styling. This cracker box, operated by Commercial Carriers, is the less common model with a setback axle. The doors on the enclosed trailer's sides provided access to the vehicles inside. *Neil Sherff*

Clark Transport Company was a carrier of Chrysler products and Cadillacs. This V-6-powered 1961 GMC tractor and Fruehauf trailer is loaded with four big 1961 Cadillacs. *Neil Sherff*

Janesville Auto Transport Company (JATCO) was the successor to W. R. Arthur and Co. This trailer was specially designed for transporting truck cabs and chassis. All five trucks in this photo are 1960 Chevrolets. *JATCO*

This is a mid-1950s Kenworth leased to Commercial Carriers. Note the condition of the front tires—they appear to be bald. The trailer is an old Western Auto Transports shop-built unit, as is the head rack. It's possible that this unit had been previously leased to Western and came along with Commercial Carriers in the buyout. *Neil Sherff*

In 1962, Studebaker produced some of these diesel tractors (model 7E45E) with a restyled front end. This one was found resting near Fisherman's Wharf in San Francisco in the late 1960s. It was operated by Greater Overseas Auto Transport. *Joseph Wanchura*

Hadley Auto Transport is the carrier operating this 1956 Ford truck and trailer. Bound for somewhere in the American Southwest is a load of 1962 Ford pickups and Falcons. *James Rowe*

The Studebaker Avanti was introduced in 1963, with a base price of $4,445. Appropriately enough, they are riding on Stuart trailers pulled by Studebaker tractors. Robert W. Walker, based in South Bend, Indiana, is the carrier.

Another Convoy Super-Duty prepares to move out with a mixed load of 1963 model vehicles. Note the all-wheel drive International Travelall, two Studebaker Larks, a Ford Fairlane, and a Plymouth Fury. The pickups are Studebaker Champs with a Lark-styled front end and a new fenderless pickup box. It really wasn't new; Studebaker bought them from an outside supplier and they were identical to the box used on the 1957 to 1960 Ford pickups. *Ackroyd Photography Inc.*

This set of turnpike doubles, loaded with 1963 Ramblers, is operated by ARCO Auto Carriers. Previously owned by the Arthurs, ARCO was sold to M. B. Troy in 1958. Troy was the builder of the Troyler trailers. These five- and six-car Troylers are pulled by a tilt cab Diamond T. *Neil Sherff*

"SK" haulaway

TRAILER SHOWN WITH SIX CADILLACS

Loads:
Six Cadillacs or smaller cars.
One car loaded on headramp.

Loaded Height:
13'3" or less depending on cars loaded.

Unit Length:
53'-8½" with 145" wheelbase, LCF tractor.
Meets axle load limits.
All structure members tubular steel.
Equipped with three hydraulic lifts.

WHITEHEAD & KALES CO.

58 HALTINER STREET • RIVER ROUGE, MICHIGAN

With many states allowing longer combinations, six-car units like this W&K SK became the norm. Note how the rear of the car sitting on the gooseneck extends almost to the back of the tractor's cab. The tractor is an 80-series Chevrolet, and the Cadillacs are 1964s. Note the limo on the rear deck.

JATCO took advantage of the longer length limits by building these seven-car stinger-steered rigs. The three-car head racks on these 1963 and 1964 Chevrolets are new but the trailers have been rebuilt, using older four-car trailers as a base. *JATCO*

Before leaving Sober's yard in Lansing, Michigan, the trucks are fueled and their height is checked. The worker at the top of the ladder is checking the height by watching the truck pass under strips of rubber of varying lengths attached to a bar. It appears that this load of 1964 Oldsmobiles is going to pass through at about 13 feet even.

Sober's maintenance people are working on two different styles of early 1960s GMCs. In the foreground is a short-hood 5000-series. Note the side-opening hood and swing-out grille panel. Behind is a conventional 4000-series tractor, on which the hood opens in a normal manner.

The intermediate size Ford, introduced in 1962, was called the Fairlane. The Fairlanes on this rig, operated by Nu Car Carriers, are 1964s. Nu Car's tractor is a 1961 Ford F-series. *Harry Patterson*

Insured Transporters served California and the Southwest and its equipment was usually impressive. This GMC cracker box is loaded with eight 1964 Chevrolet trucks. This trailer used very little in the way of hydraulics. The decks were adjusted manually before loading.

Another Southwestern GMC, this one is a 5000 model operated by Automobile Transport Company of California. There's some nice looking late model used cars in this load, including a 1962 Ford Fairlane, a 1963 Thunderbird, a 1964 Grand Prix, a 1963 Ford wagon, a 1960 Thunderbird, a 1965 Ford Galaxie, and what looks like a 1963 Buick.

Truck stop activity circa 1965. One of Anchor Motor Freight's six-car rigs with a Chevrolet tractor and loaded with 1965 Buicks, prepares to move out. In the background are two Macks, an H-model COE and a B-model, and two loads of 1965 Fords on Automobile Transport, Inc., rigs. *Harry Patterson*

Chrysler's 1965 model lineup is well represented in this nine-car load transported by Convoy. The truck chassis for this outfit is a 1963 Dodge D-800. On board are two Plymouth Belvederes, a Chrysler New Yorker, a Dodge Coronet, a Plymouth Fury III, a Plymouth Fury Suburban wagon, and three Valiants. Note the vinyl top on the New Yorker has been covered with sheet plastic for protection. *Ackroyd Photography Inc.*

The Dodge M37 3/4-ton trucks continued in military service throughout the 1960s. In this 1966 photo, Howard Sober is transporting M37s that appear to have been recently reconditioned. Sober's tractor is a new GMC 8500-series with V-6 power (gasoline). *Joseph Wanchura*

The short conventional GMC was destined to become a favorite of the auto transporters. This diesel tractor and W&K trailer are state of the art for 1966. The trailer sold for $7,250 and was equipped with air suspension. The tractor is fitted with a pusher axle with the outside tires removed. This is a test load of one 1966 Plymouth Fury I (a police car) and six Chrysler Newports. Note the car on the gooseneck is almost touching the back of the GMC cab. *Ronald Adams*

Convoy developed 10-car equipment in 1966. The tractor is a Ford N-850 diesel, with a short-hood design very similar to the GMC 5000. The load is an assortment of 1966 Ford vehicles, including a Ranchero and four Mustangs. *Ackroyd Photography Inc.*

Ford built Mustangs in several plants, including Metuchen, New Jersey. Operated by Nu Car Carriers, this Ford F-series is westbound on U.S. Route 22, with a load of 1966 Mustangs. *Ronald Adams*

This Nu Car F-950-D was one of Nu Car Carrier's first diesel tractors. Note the single tires on the pusher axle. The six-car load consists of full-size Fords destined for a big city taxi company. *Harry Patterson*

During the 1950s, Robertson Truck-A-Ways hauled Chrysler vehicles out of the West Coast assembly plants. When the plants closed, they continued to deliver Chryslers from the railheads and prep centers. Like most Chrysler carriers, Robertson's fleet included a majority of Dodges. However, there were some unusual rigs like this late 1950s Autocar. A 1966 Dodge Polara above the cab and other 1966 Chrysler products make up this load.

In the 1966 model year, Ford introduced the Bronco sport utility vehicle. It was similar in size and concept to the International Scout, introduced in 1961. The Bronco was available with a wide list of options, some of which can be seen in this photo. The two units in the bottom of the trailer, with half cabs, are called sport utility models, while the full cab models were called wagons. Automobile Transport's tractor is a 1965 Ford F-series. *Ronald Adams*

By the late 1960s, trailers needed to be adaptable to many different size autos and light commercial vehicles. With an overall length of 55 feet, this W&K trailer and Dodge LCF could transport six large autos or a combination of cars and trucks. These are 1967 Chrysler products. Note the little A-100 vans.

Where 60-foot combinations were legal, seven- and eight-car stingers could operate. This Stuart trailer and head rack, mounted on a GMC 8500 diesel chassis, is loaded with 1967 Cadillacs. The dark car, in the center of the trailer, is a front-wheel drive Eldorado. *Ronald Adams*

If an unusual car carrier was to be seen, it would probably show up out West. This early 1950s Freightliner was photographed while at rest from everyday use in 1967. Note how the upper decks swung up to allow access to the lower deck.

Convoy built and operated this 105-foot double combination in 1967. The truck heading this rig up is a Ford N-series diesel. The vehicles on the truck and first trailer are 1967 GM products, while the four autos on the second trailer are Fords. *Ackroyd Photography Inc.*

This is an early Chevrolet short-hood diesel, operated by Convoy. On board this Westland head rack and trailer is Chevrolet's 1967 lineup. Note the Chevelle SS396 convertible above the cab, two El Caminos, three Impala two-door hardtops, another Chevelle, and in the belly of the trailer, a Corvette. *Ackroyd Photography Inc.*

One of Boutell's GMCs is pictured exiting the Pennsylvania Turnpike near Carlisle, Pennsylvania, in 1967. Six new Cadillacs make up the load, transported on a W&K trailer and single-axle GMC diesel. *Ronald Adams*

Diamond T trucks were seldom seen hauling cars, but Lassiter Auto Sales ran at least one. This mid-1960s diesel appears to be undergoing minor repairs. The seven-car Stuart head rack and trailer is loaded with an assortment of mid-1960s GM products. *Joseph Wanchura*

KAT's convertible trailers grew longer and gained a tandem axle in the 1960s. Note the collection of license plates on this International BC diesel tractor. This load of used autos also includes a speedboat and trailer. *Joseph Wanchura*

PMT (Pacific Motor Trucking) was the trucking subsidiary of the Southern Pacific Railroad. Since the 1930s, it has delivered GM products from railheads and assembly plants in the Southwest. These steel tilt cab Chevrolets and GMCs were popular with PMT, and many remained in use well into the 1990s. *Joseph Wanchura*

The Dodge LCF produced in 1968 was almost identical to the truck introduced in 1960. Truck number 7777 is a Dodge CN-800, operated by Cassens. The seven-car Stuart trailer is partly empty, but the remaining units are 1968 Chrysler products. On the top deck are two Plymouth Satellites and a Dodge Coronet. Below are two Chryslers. *Ronald Adams*

Complete Auto Transit also operated seven-car Stuart equipment but with GMC 8500 chassis. The units in this load are 1968 Chevrolets. Note the Caprice two-door hardtop with its formal roofline, loaded behind the cab. *Ronald Adams*

Gasoline-powered five-car rigs were still in wide use in 1969. This 1966 Chevrolet conventional tractor is loaded with 1969 GMC and Chevrolets. *Ronald Adams*

E&L's early diesels were N-series Fords like this Cummins-powered N-1000-D. Other Ford carriers also favored the N-series because its short hood allowed them to use longer trailers. This load is made up of 1969 Thunderbirds and Lincoln Continental Mk III two-door hardtops. *Harry Patterson*

The N-series Ford was the forerunner of the Louisville model introduced in 1970. Both saw wide usage in the auto transport field. Automobile Transport, Inc., is the operator of this seven-car rig, based on a Ford N. The cars and pickup are 1969 Fords. *Ronald Adams*

For 1969, the Dodge LCF was updated with single headlights. This was the most visible change made on the LCF in its 16-year production run. This photo is a good example of just how adaptable Convoy's lightweight equipment was. The bare chassis on the trailer are Dodges, probably motor home chassis. Riding on the new Dodge CNT-800 truck are three 1969 Chrysler products—a Dodge pickup, an Imperial two-door hardtop, and a Plymouth Sport Fury. The box on the right side cowl, with the fleet number 624, is a Farr air filter. *Ackroyd Photography Inc.*

Still in service in 1969, this GMC diesel is a holdover from the 1950s. Note that the second axle on this truck is not touching the ground. It's a pusher axle and when not in use, it is raised up to reduce tire wear. It's possible that this Commercial Carriers rig is another that had previously been operated by Western. The head rack is constructed in the same manner as theirs were. *Joseph Wanchura*

This D-800 Dodge operated in western Canada is similar to the equipment that Convoy operated in the western United States. The vehicles in the load include a 1969 Dodge pickup, three Chryslers, three Dodge Darts, and a Dodge Polara. *Ackroyd Photography Inc.*

CHAPTER 6

The 1970s

Mergers and Energy Concerns

There had been mergers and buyouts in the auto transport industry since shortly after the first carriers were formed. One of the earliest mergers of a major transporter occurred in the late 1930s when Complete Auto Transit bought Driveaway Corporation of Missouri. Throughout the 1940s and 1950s, smaller companies were bought up by larger concerns and even the great Western Auto Transports proved not immune to takeover, and was purchased by Commercial Carriers.

Many of the early auto transport pioneers of the 1920s and 1930s were nearing retirement age in the late 1950s. Among them were W. R. and Hazel Arthur, in Janesville, Wisconsin. They had already sold their interests in ARCO Carriers and Dealers Transport and their only remaining auto transport holding was ownership of W. R. Arthur, in Janesville. In 1960, they sold that company to Edmund M. Brady and the company was renamed Janesville Auto Transport Company (JATCO). JATCO remained a Chevrolet contract carrier and the

equipment continued to run in Arthur's colors of mariner blue and yellow with red trim. Although Arthur had experimented with five-car rigs in the 1950s, most of his equipment remained the four-car type. One of the first things Brady did after taking over was to convert the fleet to five- and six-car rigs.

In the mid-1960s, a transportation company known as National City Lines (NCL) acquired several auto transport firms in and around the Great Lakes area. Its acquisitions included C&J Commercial Driveaway (C&J) and Automobile Carriers, Inc., both GM carriers based in Michigan, and Car Carriers, Inc., an Illinois-based Ford carrier. In 1969, after rejecting offers from other carriers, Brady entered into an agreement to sell JATCO to NCL. The sale was held up for several months by the ICC because JATCO's authority as a contract carrier duplicated many of NCL's other common carrier authorities. However, in December of 1970, the application was finally approved and control of JATCO was transferred to NCL. NCL's corporate

Steel hood GMC 8500 operated by C&J Commercial Driveaway. C&J normally hauled GM products, but this load of 1970 Fords is being transported for Car Carriers, Inc. Both car-hauling firms were owned by NCL. *Joseph Wanchura*

In the late 1960s and early 1970s, many carriers with Ford contracts changed the color of their equipment to Ford Motor Company's corporate colors of blue and white. Some carriers also went to a putty-gray color that Ford used on some of its corporate vehicles. Here, we see one of Associated Transports' Ford tractors in its old colors. The trailer has been painted in Ford's colors, and it carries the Ford logo. The six big "boats" in the load are 1970 Mercurys.

Hadley Auto Transport also adopted the Ford logo and blue-and-white paint for its equipment. This seven-car "west coast"-type rig is based on a mid-1960s Ford F-1000 Super-Duty. Note the Econoline van loaded above the cab. This was possible because the F-series cab was lower than the cab used on the N-series and the late R-model Louisville.

Seven large cars was the maximum load on the East Coast, where 50- to 55-foot length limits were still in effect in the early 1970s. Complete Auto Transit is hauling these 1970 Buicks out of GM's assembly plant in Doranville, Georgia. *Joseph Wanchura*

The German-built Opel was sold by Buick dealers. By 1970, Opel offered a variety of compact body styles. Above the GMC cab is an Opel GT, which had Corvette-like styling. Behind the GT, on the specially modified trailer, is an Opel Kadett GT. For several years in the late 1960s, Opel was the second-largest selling import auto in America, behind Volkswagen. Toyota moved into second place in 1969, and the rest is history. *Joseph Wanchura*

color was orange, and as equipment was reconditioned or replaced, JATCO's colors also became orange.

In 1973, NCL purchased Howard Sober, Inc., another GM carrier, based in Lansing, Michigan. With JATCO based in Wisconsin and the other GM carriers in Michigan, NCL decided to apply to the ICC for authority to haul autos in both directions on the same trucks, effectively eliminating deadheading. At first, the ICC was reluctant to grant NCL duplicating authority in some of these areas. However, in 1973, America experienced its first energy crisis. The commission eventually ruled that the energy conservation realized by elimination of empty back hauls was more important than the issue of duplicating authority. Subsequently, permission was granted for NCL to haul autos from Janesville to Detroit and back on the same rigs.

As a result of the first energy crisis, fuel and equipment prices increased. Because of these factors and increasing labor costs, NCL decided, in 1974, to divest itself of its auto transport holdings. The Sober operation was sold to Norman Collins and it became part of his Coltrans holdings, which also included Dixie Auto Transport. C&J and Automobile Carriers were sold to the Ralph Wilson organization, which also owned Motorcar Transport, another GM carrier in Michigan. By 1976, JATCO remained as NCL's only auto transport holding, and there were several bidders for it. Foremost among them was Ryder.

Ryder's first auto transport company was M&G Convoy, which it purchased in 1968. M&G was primarily a Chrysler carrier, based in Buffalo, and it hauled into much of the Northeast. In 1970, Ryder purchased Complete Auto Transit, a GM contract carrier, hauling out of GM assembly plants and railheads throughout the East and Midwest. In March of 1976, NCL signed an agreement to sell JATCO to Ryder, and an application was filed with the ICC. After months of protests and negotiations with the ICC, the purchase was approved, and Ryder assumed control in February of 1977. Like NCL years before, Ryder promptly applied for permission to haul autos east out of Janesville as far as Pennsylvania and return with loads from eastern plants. Permission was again forthcoming and JATCO and Complete were now able to reduce empty back hauls in those areas.

The various Anchor Motor Freight operations became part of Leaseway Transportation in the 1960s. Anchor was a major GM transporter in the Northeast and the largest auto transporter in the country for a time. Until the 1970s, its equipment was painted similar to Arthur's, dark blue and yellow. Under Leaseway's ownership, its colors became a lighter blue with yellow trim. Later, in the 1980s, the yellow trim disappeared but the light blue remained. Today, Leaseway is owned by the

In 1964 Dodge introduced a diesel COE, known as the L-1000. Chrysler haulers, like Cassens, Convoy, and Commercial Carriers, added them to their fleets. This LNT-1000, operated by Commercial Carriers, is a typical seven-car western-type rig of the early 1970s. *Joseph Wanchura*

The sales of the Jeep CJ-5 mushroomed in the 1970s. Convoy figured out how to get 11 CJs on this truck and semitrailer combination. Nine of these CJs have medallions on the fender sides, indicating that they're V-6 powered. The other two are probably powered by the F-head four-cylinder. *Ackroyd Photography Inc.*

KAT delivered International light-duty trucks, many of which were built in Springfield, Ohio. This load includes two Travelalls, three pickups, and two cab and chassis units. The tractor is an International "west coaster" dating from the late 1950s. *Joseph Wanchura*

Penske organization, and recently some white trucks have joined the older blue equipment.

Other transport companies became part of larger holding companies. KAT and Dallas & Mavis Forwarding Company became part of Jupiter Transportation Company. Cassens purchased several of its competitors, including Square Deal Cartage Company, in 1977. In

Operated by Rene's Auto Transport, this Mack B-73 is loaded with 1969 and 1970 Chevrolets, probably rentals. The Mack is powered by a Mack diesel V-8. Note the five-hole aluminum wheels.

the Northwest, Convoy expanded eastward by purchasing Turner Auto Transport in Kansas City. It also acquired Colorado Midland Transport and affiliated with Canadian Auto Carriers, the largest auto transporter in western Canada.

The larger companies that resulted from these mergers were able to transfer equipment between companies when business conditions changed. When it came time to buy equipment and supplies they could get better prices because they were able to buy in larger quantities. Convoy and Ryder even owned their own trailer-building facilities, in which equipment was also rebuilt.

The energy crises of 1973–1974 and 1979 caused turmoil with America's automobile manufacturers. Chrysler had just introduced a restyled line of full-size cars in the fall of 1973 but had to shutdown production at several plants to switch over to production of compacts. Other manufacturers' plants were temporarily idle while inventories of "gas guzzlers" backed up.

While domestic auto sales declined, sale of imports, especially Japanese imports, increased. Many auto transporters opened branch terminals in port cities, and the imports became an important source of revenue for them. Previously, the carriers looked at the imports as back haul freight, and some union drivers even refused to haul them because the back hauls paid a lesser rate. Until domestic auto sales rebounded, many transporters were forced to rely on imports to

Campers and motor homes of all sizes grew in popularity in the 1970s. Special-built trailers, resembling auto transporters, were constructed for their shipment. This F-series Ford truck and trailer is transporting nine lightweight fiberglass campers. *Harry Patterson*

The Bankhead B-series trailers were introduced in the late 1960s. By 1970, many eastern transport fleets added Bankheads to their rosters. The B-5 trailer had seven pairs of hydraulic cylinders and was very versatile. Florida Auto Convoy's B-5 and GMC 9500 tractor is shown here with a load of seven mid-1960s used cars. *Joseph Wanchura*

keep their fleets busy. Nu Car Carriers, a large eastern Ford carrier, started an Import Division and became a major carrier of Toyotas, Datsuns, Volkswagens, Mercedes-Benz, and other imports in the East. Its counterpart on the West Coast was Convoy, which transported vehicles for just about every importer at one time or another. Volkswagen opened a new assembly in Pennsylvania that had previously been owned by Chrysler but never completed. The contract for truckaway operations out of this plant went to Ryder's M&G Convoy.

In the next decade, more foreign manufacturers would open assembly plants in the United States.

In the 1970s, a new federal agency, OSHA, was created to insure that America's workers were working under the safest conditions possible. Soon after its creation, OSHA filed a Section 5-A violation against the auto transporters for a lack of scaffolding in loading and unloading areas. The Bureau of Motor Carrier Safety intervened and the violation was dropped. OSHA also ordered the transporters to require drivers to wear

United Van Lines and other moving companies maintained small fleets of auto transport trailers for shipping their customer's personal vehicles. An International CO-4000 is the tractor for this load of mixed vehicles. Note the subcompact Ford Pinto, Volkswagen, and Ford Mustang on the top decks. *Joseph Wanchura*

hardhats while loading and unloading. Many carriers issued their drivers the protective headgear, but in all but a few cases the hats were misplaced or thrown away.

The 55-foot length limit remained in effect in the East through most of the 1970s. The most common piece of equipment was a short-hood tractor and a 40- to 45-foot semitrailer. Carriers with GM contracts continued to favor Chevrolet or GMC tractors. In 1969, Ford replaced the N-series of short-hood conventionals with a new model called the Louisville. It would be the tractor of choice for Ford carriers for the next 25 years. The most popular Dodge model remained the C-model, introduced in 1960. However, in the Midwest and West, a few of the big COE Dodge L-models were seen. Partly as a result of the first fuel crisis, Dodge stopped producing heavy trucks in 1975. In

The International Fleetstar F-2000-D was produced from 1963 to 1967. This Fleetstar was still in service with ARCO in the 1970s. The trailer is 1970s Troyler with tandem axles and hydraulically operated decks.

A one-time transporter for Nash, ARCO made its money hauling imports in the company's last years. With a Troyler trailer, this sing e-axle Peterbilt is delivering Toyotas. Note the early Land Cruiser in the center of the trailer. *Harry Patterson*

By the mid-1970s, Volvo had earned a reputation for building cars that were not only durable, but safe as well. This Detroit Diesel-powered Chevrolet is trip leased for this load of Volvos. Note the P-1800 wagon on the trailer, a very rare model. *Harry Patterson*

addition, its cab design was 10 to 15 years old, and cramped compared to its competition. The Federal Motor Vehicle Safety Standard 121 (FMVSS-121) requiring antiskid air brake performance on tractors was also about to go into effect. Dodge cited the ambiguity of the standard and the expense to comply as another reason for halting production. Besides, light trucks, vans, and sport utility vehicles were selling like hot cakes, and Dodge wished to concentrate on production of those units. Long-time Chrysler carriers bought up Dodge's final production and salted them away for future use. When its stocks ran out, Cassens switched to GMCs until the mid-1980s, when it began using Internationals. A few other long-time Dodge users like Baker Driveaway bought some International Fleetstars. Convoy added Freightliners, including some low-profile COEs, to its fleet.

In 1977, International introduced its S-Series trucks and soon after added a special S-2200 Car Hauler model designed expressly for auto transporters. The Car Hauler included suspension modifications and a lower profile roof, reducing overall height. The GM tractors, Brigadier and Bruin were also available with an Auto Hauler package.

In 1971, Clark Transport Company officials asked Chrysler Corporation to build a fleet of low-cab diesel Dodge tractors. Thirty of these Dodges were eventually built, using D-series chassis and the C-model cab from the LCF. The fenders, hood, and grille were supplied from outside suppliers and were similar to those used by F.W.D. Troyler supplied the head racks and trailers. When Clark Transport ceased operations, these Dodges were purchased by other midwestern carriers. *Harry Patterson*

An ex-Convoy unit, this Fleetstar is now in use by Commercial Carriers. Note there are no nameplates or badges on this International. In the 1970s, Convoy hauled for just about every auto manufacturer and did not want to endorse any manufacturer's equipment as being superior to any other. For that reason, the identifying badges were removed. *Joseph Wanchura*

In the 1970s, Chevrolet had two intermediate models, which were best sellers, the Chevelle and the Monte Carlo. The Monte Carlo was introduced in 1970 as a personal luxury car, similar to the Pontiac Grand Prix. This load of Chevelles and Monte Carlos is transported by Jack Cooper Transports, Inc. The Chevrolet 90-series tractor is equipped with the steel "butterfly" hood. *Joseph Wanchura*

C&J Commercial Driveaway was one of the companies owned by NCL. Its corporate color for its auto transport companies was orange. Contracted primarily to GM, NCL's equipment was mostly GM-based, like this Chevrolet 90. *Joseph Wanchura*

Many of the independent carriers got their start by using second-hand equipment, like this old ex-Anchor Motor Freight trailer. The head rack is also off an old Anchor GM tractor but its been adapted to fit this Mack B-61. *Harry Patterson*

Anchor's colors of dark blue and yellow changed to light blue and yellow in the 1970s. The cab of this Chevrolet Titan 90 is still in the old dark blue, while the head rack and trailer have been painted in the new hues. This Stuart head rack and trailer have been specially built to transport nine subcompacts, like these Chevrolet Vegas. *Harry Patterson*

The seven-car rigs of the 1960s gave way to eight- and nine-car equipment in 1970. A new trailer manufacturer, Bankhead Engineering, introduced its B-series of trailer. The B quickly became one of the largest-selling trailers, especially popular with the eastern carriers. Delavan, W&K, and Stuart released "clones" of the Bankhead design, and many of these trailers served for 15 years or more. In the 1980s, hundreds of these trailers were rebuilt and updated by the carriers and many served for another 10 years.

Cottrell-Sullivan, Inc., was a Georgia-based company that began building auto transport equipment in the mid-1970s. Its products were widely accepted and the company grew, changing its name to Cottrell. Today, Cottrell is the largest manufacturer of auto transport equipment in the United States.

Use of the stinger grew and Bankhead and other manufacturers introduced 65-foot stingers for use in areas when they were permitted. In the West, Williams, Durobilt, and Stuart stingers were popular. Convoy continued building its own equipment at its trailer-building subsidiary, Westland Manufacturing. A few other western carriers purchased Westland equipment, which was some of the lightest transport equipment available. In the early 1970s, Convoy had already developed 65-foot rigs that could transport up to 13 subcompact automobiles.

Rail transport accounted for most of the long hauls in the 1970s, especially for distances greater than 500 miles. In some areas, that distance became less than 500 miles. The auto transporters were basically intermodal partners with the railroads. When the Chevrolet Vega was introduced, a new type of rail car, called the Vert-a-Pac, was introduced in which to ship it. The Vegas were shipped vertically, 30 to a single, fully enclosed rail car. The Vegas required special preparation for this type shipment and it was never expanded to other makes of autos. The development of longer, fully enclosed trilevels made the more expensive Vert-a-Pac unnecessary.

As the 1970s came to a close, there was talk in Washington about deregulating the trucking industry. In the next decade, that talk would lead to action.

Here's one of Robertson Truck-A-Ways's old Autocars still at work in 1971. These Chrysler products are en route from the prep center to the dealerships. Above the cab is a 1971 Plymouth Fury I, probably a police car, and behind it are two Plymouth Dusters and a Plymouth Cricket. The Cricket was built in England by Rootes and sold by Plymouth dealers to compete with the Pinto and Vega. After the 1973 model year, it was discontinued due to poor sales. Behind the cab is a black-and-white Plymouth Belvedere, another police car, a Plymouth Satellite Sebring Plus, and a Chrysler Newport Custom.

In 1971, M&G Convoy began painting its equipment in yellow, Ryder's corporate color. However, this nearly new Dodge CN-900, leased to M&G, is still in the older, more attractive red and yellow. Note the single 15-inch tire on the pusher axle and the yellow antislip paint on the fuel tank steps. This load of 1971 Plymouth Furys and Dodge Polaras originated in Newark, Delaware. *Joseph Wanchura*

Military vehicle shipments continued to figure in Convoy's game plan in the 1970s. Here, two loads of M38A1 Jeeps are being relocated for the U.S. Marine Corps. The tractor is a late 1960s Ford Super-Duty.

The replacement for the M38-A1 Jeep was the M151 Mutt, first built by Ford. Ten M151A2s, the improved version of the Mutt, are transported on equipment operated by Commercial Carriers. The tractor is a 1960s International DCF. *Russell MacNeil*

Judging from the sign on the side of the trailer, Auto Convoy used this Ford Louisville rig to transport Ford products exclusively. The Stuart trailer and head rack is loaded with 1972 Lincolns and Ford Thunderbirds.

In the early 1970s, the Stutz Motor Company of America began producing these luxury cars called Stutz Blackhawks. The car was designed by Virgil Exner and assembled in Italy on a Pontiac chassis. Dealer's Auto Transport of California is transporting these Blackhawks on a COE Freightliner. *Harry Patterson*

For many years, KAT transported Elgin street sweepers as back haul freight on its convertible auto trailers. There are two on this load, along with an International Travelall above the cab. The tractor, an International 4300 with a stainless steel sleeper, was International's premium conventional tractor of the 1970s. *Harry Patterson*

The W-series COE Ford was introduced in 1966 and resembled the Dodge L-1000. Auto transporters used them in areas where overall length was a concern. This seven-car stinger is operated by Associated Transports, loaded with 1972 Fords. *Joseph Wanchura*

E. T. Holsonback Motors operated this W-series Kenworth and Troyler trailer in its used car sales operation. Five Fords and a Chevelle make up this load. Note the Pinto above the cab. *Harry Patterson*

Although it's only carrying 12 imports, this Westland trailer was designed to transport 13 autos. Fleet number 644 is a Dodge LNT-1000, owned and operated by Convoy. Except for a Jaguar XK-E and a Jensen Interceptor, the vehicles in this load of imported autos are all products of the British Motor Company (BMC)—3 MG Midgets and 7 MGBs. *Ackroyd Photography Inc.*

Chevrolet's Vega was assembled in Lordstown, Ohio, where Anchor Motor Freight was one of the primary carriers. This Bankhead B-series trailer and head rack has been engineered to transport nine small autos like the Vega. Anchor's Chevrolet 90 tractor is running dual tires on the pusher axle. *Harry Patterson*

133

M&G Convoy was primarily an eastern carrier, but this Dodge CN-900 with an enclosed trailer carries Oklahoma and Texas permits. The old Dual Motors trailer was used to transport prototypes, test vehicles, or other units that required concealment. *Joseph Wanchura*

If International built it, you could probably find it in KAT's transport fleet. This International, with a Mercury sleeper, is a 1967 DC-400, which employed a large, COE cab mounted behind a conventional fiberglass hood. KAT's load is a variety of late model used cars, including Chevrolets, a 1967 Plymouth, and a Thunderbird. *Joseph Wanchura*

These promo shots for Nu Car Carriers show the three different types of business Nu Car was involved with in the 1970s. Ford Louisville tractors and Bankhead trailers are shown delivering 1971 Fords from the assembly plant, 1971 Fords and Mercurys from the railhead, and Datsuns from an East Coast port. *Nu Car Carriers*

The Le Car was a small front-wheel drive auto imported by Renault in the mid-1970s, some of the last French-built Renaults marketed in the United States. This load of 10 Le Cars was photographed in Oregon in 1976. Convoy's Westland rig is built on a Freightliner COE sleeper cab chassis. *Ackroyd Photography Inc.*

Medium-duty trucks were delivered by both driveaway and truckaway, as shown here. Auto Convoy is using a Ford Louisville with a tag axle to pull this specially built truck transporter.

After the energy crisis of 1973–1974, Japanese imports began selling like hotcakes. Datsun's B-210 cars and Little Hustler pickups were especially popular. This load of Datsuns is loaded on a GMC 9500 tractor and Troyler trailer operated by ARCO. *Ronald Adams*

Toyota was Datsun's rival in the early 1970s. These tractors, owned by brokers and leased to Automobile Transport, Inc., are pulling Troylers loaded with Toyotas. The trucks are, from left to right, a Ford Louisville, a Ford N-series diesel, and a Dodge CN-800 diesel. *Russell MacNeil*

Honda was a latecomer in imported autos, but quickly established a reputation for reliability and economy. ARCO was a contractor for Honda, and this Peterbilt is hauling a load west through Pennsylvania on I-78. *Ronald Adams*

The sporty Ford Capri was built in both England and Germany and sold well, through Mercury dealers, in the United States. This load was imported through the port of Baltimore, Maryland, and transported by Automobile Transport, Inc. The tractor is a Dodge CN-900 diesel. *Harry Patterson*

The Volkswagen Super Beetle was the last version of the Beetle sold in the United States. This photo, taken in 1972, shows seven Super Beetles on a Florida Auto Convoy GMC. Note the twin mufflers. *Joseph Wanchura*

Fiat had been importing autos into the United States since the 1950s. Competition from Japanese autos forced Fiat to withdraw from the U.S. in the 1980s. These Fiat 128s have been processed through an East Coast port and are being delivered by Clark Transport on one of their special-built Dodges. *Joseph Wanchura*

Sixty-foot stingers, like this Stuart, could handle eight-vehicle combinations. Auto Convoy is the operator of this Ford, loaded with eight 1972 Ford products. Note how the pickups on the head rack overlap.

These trucks, a 60-series tractor and a Titan 90 COE, are operated by Chevrolet Engineering. The 1972 Chevrolets on the Stuart trailer are probably show cars or test vehicles. A 427-cid V-8 powers the C-60, while the Titan, a clone of the GMC Astro is Detroit Diesel powered. *Joseph Wanchura*

Like Anchor, M&G Convoy also ran single tires on its pusher axles. This almost new CN-900 is loaded with 1972 Chrysler products. Note the Dodge Demon in the belly of the trailer and the Dodge Challenger above it.

One of Boutell's GMCs with a load of mixed (new and used) 1971 and 1972 Pontiacs. The GMC is a tilt hood 9500 diesel, pulling a W&K trailer from the late 1960s. *Neil Sherff*

After M&G's takeover by Ryder, its fleet color changed from red to yellow. This Dodge CN-900 is not fitted with a third axle and is pulling a low-side Delavan trailer. These trailers were designed to transport vans and pickups, but this load is 1972 Dodge and Plymouth full-size models. *Harry Patterson*

The trailers developed in the late 1960s and 1970s made greater use of hydraulic lifts. On trailers like this Bankhead, the top decks were loaded first and unloaded last. Two vehicles have already been unloaded from this rig; four 1975 Mercurys and a Lincoln remain. *Russell MacNeil*

Auto Convoy used gasoline-powered tractors, like these Fords, for local deliveries. These 1973 Ford products are being loaded at a railhead. Note the imported Ford Courier on the head rack of the last tractor in line. Close examination will also reveal an International pickup on the third trailer from the left.

Custom vans became popular in the 1970s. Although the "Big Three" offered some factory-built custom vans, most were further customized by outside firms. These Ford Econolines have had the full custom treatment, with chrome wheels, custom paint, and porthole windows. They are being transported on a 1950s Kenworth "narrow nose." *Harry Patterson*

Chevrolet introduced the Monte Carlo in 1970. The first restyle for the personal luxury car occurred in 1973. Four Monte Carlos are in this load of 1974 Chevrolets, transported by Anchor Motor Freight. *Joseph Wanchura*

The Volkswagen Rabbit replaced the Beetle in the U.S. market. Unlike the Beetle, the Rabbit was water cooled and front-wheel drive. This COE Dodge, formerly owned by Robertson Truck-A-Ways, is now operated by Commercial Carriers.

As a carrier for Ford, Automobile Transport, Inc., used Ford tractors whenever possible. However, the cab height of the Ford Louisville made hauling pickups above the cab difficult. The International Fleetstar, with its lower cab, was better suited for hauling pickups. This Fleetstar is pulling a Bankhead trailer, also specially constructed for hauling pickups. The Ford trucks are 1973 or 1974s, destined for the U.S. Navy. *Russell MacNeil*

The auto transport companies seldom haul farm equipment. That job requires specially built transport trailers like this one, operated by Reigle Express, Inc. The COE tractor is a Kenworth K-100. *Harry Patterson*

In some parts of the country, Commercial Carriers employed brokers, who operated a variety of equipment. This GMC Astro 95 sleeper makes for a very high cab. The vehicles on the top deck are Jeep Wagoneers, while below are three AMC autos.

Thrill show operators used auto transport trailers to move their equipment between shows. The Hell Drivers appear to have favored Chrysler products. Riding on an old four-car trailer that has been stretched is a Plymouth Satellite, two Valiants, and two Dodge Darts. The tractor is a 1972 Dodge D-800. *Harry Patterson*

This is Cassens with a load of 1973 Plymouth Satellites and Dodge Tradesman vans. Cassens' truck is a 1969 Dodge CN-800 with a Stuart trailer and head rack. *Joseph Wanchura*

GM's intermediate cars sold very well in the 1970s, especially the Oldsmobile Cutlass and the Pontiac LeMans. This eight-car load of Pontiacs includes a LeMans above the cab and a personal luxury Grand Prix behind the cab. The tractor is a GMC 9500 diesel.

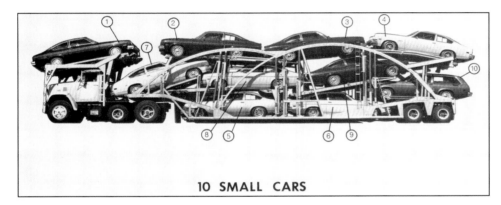

10 SMALL CARS

Cottrell-Sullivan introduced these humped style trailers in the mid-1970s. Anchor Motor Freight and Nu Car Carriers were among the carriers that purchased them in volume. This publicity shot shows how 10 Chevrolet Vegas could be packed in.

Colorado Midland Transport (CMT) is the operator of this 1950s Kenworth loaded with new and used vehicles. CMT was acquired by Convoy in 1975. The auto above the cab is a 1974 Plymouth Satellite Custom. *Harry Patterson*

This owner-operator, leased to KAT, has stopped at the Port of Entry in Cheyenne, Wyoming, in 1974. Above the Autocar's cab is an International four-wheel drive pickup, while behind the cab is a Jeep pickup. Also visible is an AMC Matador, a Dodge van, and a Jeep CJ-5. *Harry Patterson*

143

After a false start in the U.S. market in the late 1960s, Subaru introduced a line of larger front-wheel drive compacts in the early 1970s. One of Convoy's Dodge LNT-1000 rigs is seen here partially loaded with 1974 Subarus. Note the absence of nameplates on the Dodge. *Joseph Wanchura*

This KAT Freightliner COE is loaded with a wide variety of mid-1970s vehicles, including a Dodge four-wheel drive pickup, a Datsun Z-car and two B-210s, two Peugeots, a Jeep CJ-5, and a Jeep wagon. *Harry Patterson*

Like other Ford carriers, Convoy began using the Ford Louisville shortly after its introduction. This LNT-9000 and Westland FE trailer is loaded with 1974 Fords. Beginning in 1973, Convoy started painting its truck cabs white. *Ackroyd Photography Inc.*

Because Boutell's primary customer was GM, most of its equipment was GM sourced. This GMC 9500 tractor and Stuart trailer is loaded with Cadillacs. Note the midsized Seville behind the cab.

In Oklahoma and the Midwest, United Transports was GM's carrier. This steel hood GMC is loaded with eight 1977 Chevelles. United was later taken over by Jack Cooper Transports.

North of the border, Roadway Transport Limited was one of Canada's biggest carriers. One of its GMC 9500s is seen here loaded with an assortment of 1977 Chevrolets. Note the large fuel tank on the tractor.

The W&K trailer shown here is a copy of the Bankhead B-series trailers. It's pulled by a Freightliner COE, operated by Bill Garlic Motors, Inc. Note the small tires on the pusher axle. *Harry Patterson*

In February of 1975, Ford introduced restyled Econoline and Club Wagon models with longer front ends. Five of the new vans are seen here on a Stuart trailer, built expressly for hauling them. Automobile Transport's tractor is a Ford F-series. *Ronald Adams*

Convoy also used the W-series Ford COE with its lightweight Westland trailers. This nine-car combination is loaded with eight 1973 Fords. The four-wheel drive pickup in the center of the load is taking up two positions. *Ackroyd Photography Inc.*

The first Mitsubishi-built vehicles sold in this country were sold as Dodge Colts. Unlike the British-built Plymouth Cricket, the Colt proved to be durable and quite reliable. Eventually, Chrysler and Mitsubishi formed a partnership and a complete line of Dodge and Plymouth subcompact vehicles were marketed. This Robertson Truck-A-Ways Dodge CNT-900 is loaded with eight 1974 Colts. The truck is a 1968, the last year the C-model had four headlights. *Russell MacNeil*

In 1973, Ford gave the W-series COE a grille similar to the one used on the Louisville. This W-series, operated by Hadley Auto Transport, was still at work in the late 1980s. *James Rowe*

In addition to autos, light trucks, and boats, KAT also hauled heavy-duty trucks. This Mack Cruiseliner is transporting two Kenworth gliders. The Cruiseliner was introduced in 1974 as a replacement for the Mack F-model COE. However, both models were sold side by side for a while. A glider is a new truck built without an engine, transmission, or rear axles. The buyer supplies this item from an existing truck. *Harry Patterson*

Car-hauling accidents happen, as seen here. This Dodge Aspen wagon has run out of its track and is suspended between two decks. This is a minor incident, easily rectified, although there may be some undercarriage damage to the Aspen.

In August 1977, Convoy purchased its first "low silhouette" Freightliner. It was the only auto transporter of its type in the country at that time. Convoy was Freightliner's biggest low silhouette truck customer for the next three years. However, in 1980, Freightliner stopped production of this unit. Convoy then turned to Kenworth and Peterbilt for additional low silhouette units.

The GMC 9500 became the Brigadier in 1978, with a new squared-off hood. This Brigadier, operated by C&J Commercial Driveaway, is hauling Alfa Romeos.

Peterbilt COE trucks were rarely seen in use as auto transporters, but this one is an exception. Leased to Commercial Carriers, it's loaded with 1979 Chrysler and AMC vehicles, Dodge pickups, and B-series wagons on top and Dodge Omnis and an AMC Spirit on the bottom.

This assortment of nine 1979 GM vehicles is preparing to leave JATCO's yard in Janesville, Wisconsin. Note how far the Camaro on the lower deck hangs out to the rear. Above it is a 1979 Corvette.

JATCO's older equipment, like this Chevrolet 90 and early Bankhead trailer, was still in use in 1979. The mixed GM load includes four pickups. Note that a pickup could legally be transported above the Chevrolet cab.

The popularity of vans and sport utility vehicles led to the development of equipment that would transport them efficiently. The Delavan 2500 was a 43-foot long trailer designed for this purpose. The overall length of these units was 55 feet. Later, these trailers were lengthened to 53 feet.

Compared to the Ford L-model, the GM tractor's cabs were several inches lower. For that reason, Nu Car Carriers added a few GM tractors to its fleet. This one, hauling a Ford Pinto, has had its nameplates removed. It could be a GMC or Chevrolet.

Ryder standardized on Delavan's 2600 trailer in the late 1970s. Its versatility is shown in this series of photos. The tractors are all Chevrolets, 90-series or Bruins.

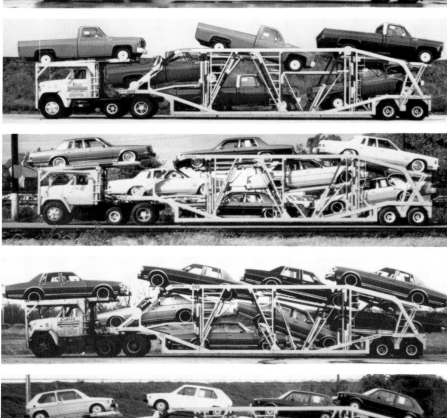

GMC, AN AUTO TRANSPORT FAVORITE

For most of the years that the GMC nameplate appeared on heavy trucks, they were the most popular auto transport tractors. They were not only popular with the GM haulers, but other carriers sometimes had some GMCs in their fleets. Throughout the 1950s, most of these units were gasoline-powered models. Insured Transporters, in California, used some diesel GMCs in the late 1950s and more than one broker leased to KAT and other carriers had GMC diesels on the road. In 1962, a new short-hood diesel GMC was introduced, and with it came a Chevrolet version, which used the medium-duty GM cab with a new shortened front end.

In 1966, GM again introduced a new line of medium and heavy trucks that would become the auto transporter's favorite for the next 25 years. These trucks, featuring a distinctive "fish nose" styling with a new roomier cab, were eventually available with two different hood lengths, including a shorter 92-inch hood that was perfect for car-hauling applications. Both gasoline and diesel engines were available, but the diesel was most popular in the heavy-duty models. The GMC division built both the GMC and Chevrolet models, and their technical model numbers were similar. In the marketplace, they were known as Heavy-Duty Conventionals; Chevrolets were called C-80 and

In the 1950s, GMCs like this model 450 COE were extensively used by auto transport companies. Most of these tractors were powered by the GMC 302 gasoline engine. Before 1960, only a few carriers operated GMC diesel-powered tractors.

152

The short-hood GMCs were introduced in the early 1960s, just as the diesel's popularity was increasing. This GMC 5000 diesel, leased to Dallas & Mavis Forwarding Company, is loaded with 1968 Jeep vehicles. Harry Patterson

This is a GMC version of the heavy-duty conventional introduced by GM in 1966. The fiberglass hood tilted forward for ease of servicing. On this unit, the front fenders have been narrowed so that they will pass between the head rack's uprights when tilted. This load of 1968 GMCs includes one Handy-Van. Joseph Wanchura

The short-hood Chevrolets were almost identical to the GMCs, usually differing only in the grille treatment. This late 1960s served JATCO for almost 15 years.

C-90s, while GMCs were called 8500 or 9500s. In styling, they differed only in grille treatments and badging.

Shortly after the new conventionals were introduced, the auto transporters with GM contracts began adding them to their fleets. In addition to their short bumper to back of cab (BBC) dimensions, these trucks had a relatively low cab height. This was very important to auto transporters and enabled them to legally transport light trucks and vans on the head racks of these vehicles. This was not the case with the Ford Louisville tractor, introduced in 1969. Many Ford carriers found that they could not transport tall vehicles over the cab of the Ford tractor. For that reason, some Ford carriers purchased limited numbers of the GM conventionals for use at locations where large numbers of tall vehicles were shipped.

Production of the GM conventionals continued into the 1970s with only slight changes in the vehicles. Larger, more powerful diesel engines were offered in the early 1970s, requiring that the cab be raised higher off the chas-sis. In 1978, a more angular fiberglass nose assembly was introduced, and the trucks were renamed. The GMC model became the Brigadier, while the Chevrolet was called Bruin. The Brigadier would continue in production through 1988, when Volvo-White took over GM Heavy Truck and renamed the GMCs WHITEGMCs. Production of the Bruin stopped in the 1980 model year, when Chevrolet quit marketing heavy trucks. Brigadiers and Bruins remained in use with some auto transporters through the 1980s and beyond. A few can still be seen today.

Shortly after Volvo-White took over GM Heavy Truck, it introduced a replacement for the Brigadier, the WG. In most cases, carriers who used Brigadiers found the WG to be a suitable replacement. Originally the higher cab height of the WG was found to be a problem and a special "car hauler" version was developed with a lower cab. Today, the WGs are marketed under the Volvo name and are among the most popular auto transport tractors.

The later model Chevrolet 90s used the GMC grille with a Chevrolet nameplate and bow tie. This 1973 tractor is equipped with a W&K three-car head rack. Note the huge fuel tank for the thirsty Detroit diesel motor.

After Dodge stopped producing heavy-duty trucks in 1975, Chrysler carriers had to look to other manufacturers for equipment. M&G Convoy went to GM tractors, like this GMC 9500 with a pusher or "tag" axle. Note the holes in the front bumper, which allow increased airflow to the radiator.

The GM conventionals were restyled and renamed in 1978. Brigadier was the name selected for the new square nose GMC. This load of Saabs, pulled by a Brigadier, is leaving the Dundalk Marine Terminal in Baltimore, Maryland, in 1987.

The Chevrolet version of the Brigadier was called Bruin. Again, it differed only in its grille treatment. This Bruin, an ex-Anchor Motor Freight tractor, is shown unloading Subarus in the early 1990s.

In the late 1970s, Anchor's rigs lost their yellow trim and were painted overall in Leaseway's corporate light blue. Note the square opening in the front bumper of this GMC Brigadier operated by Anchor. Visible inside this opening is a pintle hook, similar to the one on the rear of a semitrailer used in a double combination. When Leaseway operated doubles on eastern turnpikes, this pintle hook was used to move the second trailer around the parking areas. *Allen Neamtz*

The 2311 was Delavan's 65-foot stinger, developed in the 1970s. In 1978, the 2311 was combined with the Chevrolet Bruin tractor and became Ryder's standard stinger. This is a test load of 10 Volkswagen Rabbits. Note the four pickups.

Broker-owned Dodges remained in M&G's fleet long after the company-owned Dodges were retired. This early 1970s CN-900 was based in Newark, Delaware, hauling Chrysler vehicles from the railhead and assembly plant there. The Delavan trailer has been modified to haul eight units, with one more above the cab.

CHAPTER 7

The 1980s

Deregulation and Consolidation

As America entered the 1980s, the domestic automobile industry was still in turmoil. Chrysler was on the brink of financial failure with its only hope for the future resting on the soon to be introduced K-Car. By the mid-1980s, the most popular American autos were fuel-efficient, four-cylinder models.

In the auto transport industry, mergers and buyouts continued. Ryder acquired Boutell in 1981 and Commercial Carriers in 1982. Both companies had contracts with GM and the importers, while Commercial Carriers also transported for Chrysler and American Motors Corporation in some parts of the country. Ryder also purchased Fleet Carrier Corporation and Convoy, along with its subsidiaries. In Canada, Ryder

purchased Motor Carriers Limited (MCL) and Auto Carriers Limited (ACL); GM's dedicated carriers in eastern Canada. With these acquisitions, Ryder became a nationwide carrier, with terminals in every region.

Leaseway Transportation also expanded in the 1980s with the purchase of several carriers, including C&J Commercial Driveaway in Lansing, Michigan, and Nu Car Carriers. Nu Car was primarily a Ford carrier in the East. For the first time in recent history, Leaseway had extensive contracts with Ford Motor Company. Possibly because of Leaseway's close association with GM, Ford did not renew many of Nu Car's contracts when it was time to renew them in the late 1980s. Most were awarded to two other Ford carriers,

The early 1980s were the last days for Boutell. Taken over by Ryder, its equipment, like the GMC Brigadier, was distributed to Ryder's other operations such as M&G and Complete Auto Transit. *Ronald Adams*

The last model year for the Plymouth Volare was 1980. In the final years of its short, five-year production run, a few were built as police cars. Three Volare police cars are in this load about to be unloaded from this Delavan 2600 trailer, operated by M&G. The tractor is a GMC 9500 diesel.

Checker had been building taxicabs since the 1920s. In 1956, it introduced the Marathon, which continued in production virtually unchanged through 1982. Flynn Motors' GMC 9500 and Bankhead trailer is loaded with two Checkers and a Chevrolet Chevette.
Harry Patterson

For moving equipment between terminals or sending it off for servicing, M&G removed the head rack from an old Dodge CN-900 and hooked it up to a shop-built flat-bed trailer. The tractors on the trailer are GMC Brigadiers.

Allied Systems Ltd. and E&L Transport, while Ryder also picked up a few.

Two southern carriers, the Motor Convoy in Atlanta, and the Auto Convoy in Dallas, combined to form Allied Systems in 1986. For two years, they continued to operate with their own separate headquarters, but in 1988, they consolidated their operations base in Atlanta and dropped their individual names. When the consolidation was complete, Allied Systems became the third-largest auto carrier in the United States.

In the West, Jack Cooper Transports took over United Transports and PMT, the Southern Pacific's highway auto-hauling division. By the end of the 1980s, only a few of the original auto transporters were not part of a larger company.

Many of the mergers of the 1980s came about because of deregulation. There was a lot of talk about deregulation in the 1970s, but it became a reality in 1980 when Congress passed the Motor Carrier Act of 1980, deregulating the trucking industry. Deregulation eliminated most of the restrictions that were imposed by the Motor Carrier Act of 1935. Carriers were now free to serve any and all shippers and rates were no longer regulated. The auto makers were now able to solicit competitive bids from as many carriers as wished to bid. As a result, many carriers now operated in areas well beyond the limits of their old ICC rights. Several carriers, among them Cassens and Jack Cooper, bid on and received work that had previously been handled by the railroads.

Loads out of assembly plants in Missouri and Illinois were shipped via truck as far as eastern Pennsylvania and New York, a distance of 800 miles or more. The dealers were delighted, as they received autos within a

Eight Pontiac Firebirds and Chevrolet Camaros on a late 1970s Delavan 65-foot stinger. These GMC 9500-based rigs served the various Ryder companies well throughout the 1980s.

American intermediate cars shrunk in size in the late 1970s and early 1980s. This load, transported by Budget Car Rental, includes two Chevrolet Monte Carlos, two Pontiac Grand Prixs, a Ford Fairmont, and a Chevrolet Impala. Budget's tractor is a Ford F-series. *Michael Haeder*

few days of their build date. The drivers, who were paid by the mile, also liked the long hauls. However, in most cases, the midwestern companies were unable to secure back hauls from East Coast plants and most of their trucks were returning empty. Jack Cooper's trucks did get a limited number of loads out of the GM plants in New Jersey, Delaware, and Maryland, but most of Cassens' trucks deadheaded home. After the Teamsters strike of 1985, the railroads were able to recover many of these long hauls.

Deregulation allowed new carriers to start up, many with only one truck. No longer was there a requirement for a carrier to petition the ICC and have his petition subject to protests of other carriers. In most cases these smaller, nonunion companies served the auto auction industry and leasing companies. Although the Big Three and most importers continued to use union carriers, a few of the smaller, nonunion companies were able to get some smaller import contracts.

On the heels of deregulation came the Surface Transportation Act of 1982. This act increased and standardized weight, length, and width limits on the Interstate Highway System. In exchange for these standards, the trucking industry agreed to increased taxes. Unfortunately, the individual states continued to regulate size limits on roads other than interstates. Some state and local regulations still differ from the federal standards, but today the 75-foot stinger is allowed in most areas.

The sales of Japanese autos increased in the early 1980s and American auto makers tried to get the American public to "buy American." As a result, the Japanese made plans to follow Volkswagen's lead and establish assembly plants in the United States. Nissan opened its first U.S. assembly plant here in Smyrna, Tennessee, in 1982. The major truckaway carrier there was Coltrans' Dixie Auto Transport. Dixie was made up primarily of brokers pulling trailers owned or on lease to Dixie's parent company, Coltrans. Many of their hauls were very long with a limited number of back hauls. At times, the volume of traffic out of Smyrna was more than Dixie could handle, requiring Nissan to temporarily contract

Ryder's 55-foot rigs could also transport eight Firebirds or Camaros, as this 1982 shot shows. Complete Auto Transit's tractor is a GMC Brigadier.

Convoy operated a large number of Freightliner tractors. Compare the cab height of the low-profile model on the left with the standard COE day cab on the right. The standard COE is too high for a pickup to be carried above the cab.
Mark Waterman

The smaller GM intermediates continued to sell very well in the 1980s. This load includes four intermediate Oldsmobile Cutlass models and three full-size Oldsmobiles. The Bankhead B-6 trailer is hooked up to a GMC Brigadier. *Russell MacNeil*

Commercial Carriers acquired some low-profile Freightliners in the late 1970s. This one with a Williams trailer and head rack had previously been owned by Robertson Truck-A-Ways.

with other carriers to alleviate backlogs. Shortly after the Teamsters strike in 1985, Nissan dropped Dixie and contracted with Cassens, The Auto Convoy, and Nu Car Carriers for the traffic out of Smyrna. Dixie continued to haul imported autos out of the East Coast ports but its financial condition was beginning to deteriorate. Without domestic contracts, Dixie had no source of income hauling autos at full rate. In the mid-1980s, the imports continued to pay a lesser rate than the domestic autos.

Honda began producing Accords at a new plant in Marysville, Ohio, in September of 1983. Originally, Honda contracted with four different carriers at Marysville but eventually the number declined to just two, Cassens and Commercial Carriers. They remain the truckaway carriers out of Marysville today, although Commercial Carriers is now part of Allied Systems.

Toyota, Mitsubishi, and other Japanese auto makers opened assembly plants here and in Canada. Some were joint ventures with American auto makers, like the Toyota-GM plant in California and Nissan-Ford plant in Ohio. In many cases, auto transporters gained work out of these plants to offset the work lost because of domestic plant closings.

After opening its plant in Pennsylvania, Volkswagen began work on a second facility in Sterling Heights, Michigan, north of Detroit. However, while sales of Japanese imports increased, Volkswagen's sales leveled off and even began to decline. When it became apparent that the plant would not be needed, Volkswagen halted the plant's construction.

On the brink of bankruptcy in the early 1980s, Chrysler had closed several of its old, inefficient Detroit plants such as Hamtramck and Lynch Road Assembly.

The Fiero was a mid-engined sports car built and sold by Pontiac in the mid-1980s. The first Fieros were available only in red, as seen on this Anchor rig moving eastbound through Pennsylvania. The other vehicles in the load are Oldsmobile Cutlass two-doors. Anchor's mid-1970s GMC diesel is outfitted with a Bankhead trailer and head rack. *Ronald Adams*

Roadway Transport Limited transported GM vehicles from assembly plants and marshaling yards in Canada to dealers in Eastern Canada. In the mid-1980s, Roadway's name was changed to "Auto Carriers Limited ACL." The early 1980s Brigadier and Stuart trailer is hauling Chevrolet Impalas and Pontiac 6000s in the days before the name change.

The Renault Alliance was the *Motor Trend* Car of the Year for 1983. The Alliance and a smaller Encore were designed by Renault but built in AMC's Kenosha, Wisconsin, assembly plant. KAT was one of AMC's primary carriers. This load of Kenosha-built Renaults is transported on a Mack R-model, operated by KAT's sister company, Dallas & Mavis Forwarding Company. *Ronald Adams*

Brokers or owner-operators leased to KAT and Dallas & Mavis operated a variety of equipment. However, as in years past, most were Internationals. This Transtar C-O F4070A dates from the early 1970s and was still in use in 1985. The trailer is the 48-foot Bankhead, of which KAT acquired several hundred in the early 1980s.

By 1983, Chrysler's sales were increasing and it needed additional production capacity. This time, Chrysler bought Volkswagen's unfinished Sterling Heights plant and earmarked it as the production site for two new K-Car variants it was about to introduce. Production of the Chrysler Lebaron GTS and the Dodge Lancer began in late 1984. Unlike the 1950s, when there were almost 80 carriers hauling for Chrysler, two carriers, M&G and Cassens, hauled most of Chrysler's vehicles that were produced in Michigan. These carriers figured that they'd be "shoo-ins" at Sterling Heights also. However, when the contract was awarded, it went to Leaseway Motorcar Transport, a carrier who had never hauled for Chrysler before. In fact, except for a few import autos, Leaseway had been a dedicated GM carrier and a division of Leaseway Transportation. Soon after Leaseway began operations out of Sterling Heights, it was also awarded other Chrysler contracts in the East. This work involved hauling out of newly established railheads, and from others that had been served by M&G. After about 10 years, the Sterling Heights contract was rebid and awarded to Cassens. Leaseway went back to hauling primarily for GM and a few importers.

This load of mid-1980s Nissans is being moved by a Kenworth conventional and Cottrell trailer. Note, this Cottrell trailer has three humps, unlike the two-hump model more commonly seen. Above the Kenworth's cab is a Maxima station wagon and behind it is a Z car. *Harry Patterson*

163

The S-series International was introduced in 1977 and a special Car Hauler model was developed. This S-2200, operated by Auction Transport, is equipped with a Delavan 65-foot stinger trailer and four-car head rack. Note the 1955 Cadillac above the cab.

MCL (Motor Carriers Limited), a dedicated GM carrier in Canada, operated this specially constructed Chevrolet Bruin and flat trailer designed to transport cab and chassis units. Note this tractor has a tag axle with small wheels behind the drive axle.

This is another of MCL's special rigs. Built to transport vehicles requiring maximum protection or concealment, this 48-foot Autohaul trailer is pulled by a GMC General tractor. Note the lowered rear door, which doubles as a loading ramp.

The unstable domestic auto market of the late 1970s and early 1980s provided many carriers with a surplus of equipment. Consequently, new equipment purchases were down. In 1979, Automobile Transport, Inc., a large Ford carrier, ceased operations. Other midwestern and eastern carriers purchased much of their equipment. Shortly after changing its name to Alpha-X in the late 1970s, Baker Driveaway also went out of business. Throughout the 1980s, it was common to see old Baker and Alpha-X equipment rusting away in fields in the Maryland countryside. The big carriers like Leaseway and Ryder had a huge variety of surplus equipment acquired in mergers and takeovers.

As domestic auto sales rebounded in 1983 and 1984, many carriers required additional equipment to handle the increased shipments. With new, longer, federal length limits now in effect, the 65- and 75-foot stingers were now legal in most areas. Many eastern fleets purchased a few, sometimes only for use as test units.

There were still hundreds of the Bankhead B-model trailers in use across the country that had been built in the early 1970s. Although structurally sound, they were shorter than the newer models, which measured between 48- and 53-feet long. Cottrell, a large auto transport manufacturer in Georgia, initiated a rebuild program that modernized the decks and increased the length on these units and others. This trailer was well received by several carriers. Nu Car Carriers had hundreds rebuilt, and these units became its standard trailers in the mid-1980s. Many can still be seen in use by independent carriers today

In addition to using Delavan trailers, Ryder also had also acquired large numbers of old Bankheads and Stuarts when it bought JATCO and Boutell. Delavan, Ryder's trailer-building subsidiary, developed several rebuild programs to improve and modernize these units. Many trailers were stretched to 48- and 53-foot lengths. In 1986, Delavan developed a quickloader trailer, based on old Bankhead B-6 and Delavan Model 2600 trailers. These trailers were lengthened and the top decks were completely reconfigured to allow quicker loading and

The Western Star was a premium tractor seldom used by auto transporters. This one, operated by a broker and leased to Dixie Auto Transport, is hauling 1984 Nissans built in Smyrna, Tennessee. The trailer is a new 48-foot Stuart.
Ronald Adams

The low cab height of the GM tractors permitted large vehicles, like these full-size Dodge vans, to be carried above the cab. This load, shot in Newark, Delaware, in 1985, is transported on a Stuart trailer built especially for transporting these kinds of vehicles. The tractor is a GMC 9500 diesel from the mid-1970s.

By the mid-1980s, most Ford carriers were using the Ford L-models. Hadley tried a few of these F-800 diesels with Williams trailers and head racks and found their lower cab height to be an advantage. *James Rowe*

unloading. The following year, Delavan offered this trailer commercially and many were sold to other eastern carriers. It too, remains very popular with the independents and used car dealers.

Leaseway's rebuild program involved converting older high-mount fifth wheel Brigadier and Bruin tractors into stingers. These were combined with Cottrell's CS-10 trailers, and they served Leaseway into the mid-1990s. These rebuilds were a less complex model of the standard Cottrell stinger in use by many carriers in the 1980s. Even though most carriers rebuilt or purchased new equipment in the 1980s, it was still possible to see 15- to 20-year old rigs hauling autos, especially in the West.

Fully enclosed auto transport trailers had been in limited use since the 1930s. Most carriers had a few which were used for transporting special cargo such as show cars, prototypes, or limited production units. The

Several carriers served the Marysville, Ohio, Honda plant, where these Accords were built. Cassens and Commercial Carriers eventually became the exclusive carriers there. This low-profile Freightliner and Williams trailer, operated by Commercial Carriers, was an ex-West Coast rig. *Ronald Adams*

The success of the Mercedes-Benz/Lohr units led Nu Car to order larger Lohr trailers combined with Ford LNT-9000 tractors. About a dozen were built at Lohr USA in 1986. They were used to transport smaller vehicles like Ford Escorts and Nissans, as shown here.

In the mid-1980s, the Canadian carriers were allowed 70 feet overall length and 14 feet, 6 inches of height. This mid-1970s Chevrolet 90 and Bankhead trailer, operated by MCL has been converted to haul 8 to 10 vehicles and still conform to those requirements. Note there is no overhang on these GM vehicles.

The Ford Tempo and Mercury Topaz were Ford's midsize cars introduced in the 1980s. E&L is transporting this load on a Cottrell humped trailer, pulled by an International S-2200 Car-Hauler tractor. Note the short wheelbase of this tractor. *Allen Neamtz*

Auto Haulaway was a large Canadian carrier operating a wide variety of equipment. This 10-year-old Ford W-series was still at work in August 1986, hauling full-size Fords west on Highway 401 in Ontario.

In the early 1980s, GMC offered a slope hood version of the Brigadier as an option. Ryder's future purchases were equipped with this option, which came with a smaller grille. This one, operated by M&G, is a Delavan 10-car rig, which was the older 2311 style trailer, combined with a 4-car head rack tractor. Even though it was called a 10-car, 7 pickups and vans fill it to capacity.

This Ryder Brigadier is a West Coast type rig. Unlike the eastern GMCs with cast spoke wheels and Bankhead or Delavan head racks, the western equipment had Budd wheels and W&K or Williams head racks. Quick-load trailers also appeared earlier in the West. This load of 1986 GM vehicles was shot in Idaho. *James Rowe*

In 1985, Delavan introduced the 11-car Model 2800. It used the 4-car head rack and a low side trailer. Several hundred of these rigs were put in service with the various Ryder companies across the country. This 11-car rig, operated by Complete Auto Transit, is loaded with mail van chassis.

Although the Brigadier was the most common Ryder tractor in the 1980s, a few GMC Astro 95s were built up into 11-car 2800s. Because of the Astro's high cab, the 4-car head rack was seldom used.

Full-size Dodge vans and wagons were built in Windsor, Ontario, at Chrysler's Pillette Road Plant. Cassens used this GMC Brigadier and special trailer (and others like it) to transport finished vans to Detroit, where they would be put into loads to destinations in the United States. This truck would make several trips across the Ambassador Bridge from Windsor to Detroit each day.

Leaseway Motorcar Transport began hauling Chrysler vehicles out of the CSX railhead located in Jessup, Maryland, in 1985. Its equipment, seen here, was ex-Anchor Motor freight Chevrolet Bruins and Cottrell humped trailers. The vehicles on these rigs are 1987 Chryslers.

Commercial Carriers employed brokers or owner-operators at several of its terminals. This 1983 GMC General was owned by Freddie Nelson and leased to Commercial in Chicago. When this photo was taken, it was loaded with used cars. Above the cab is a 1966 Ford LTD, while on the trailer are two Lincoln Versailles, a Mark III, a Chevy Nova, a Ford pickup, and a Tempo or Topaz. *Freddie Nelson*

Magirus entered the U.S. truck market in the late 1970s and at least one of its trucks went into service hauling cars. CTC (Car Transporters Corp.) had this Magirus fitted with a head rack and trailer similar to those used on its Freightliners. This shot shows a load of Porsche and Audi vehicles.

In the 1970s, PMT purchased hundreds of these diesel-powered GMC tilt cabs. By the time this photo was taken in 1986, those that were still in use were used for local deliveries. The over-the-road hauls were performed by newer equipment, usually GMC Brigadiers. *Fred Yokel*

Although most new vehicle shipments were handled by a handful of big companies, a few smaller companies, like Ravenna Transport, had contracts to haul imports. This load of 1987 Subarus is shown leaving the Dundalk Marine Terminal, in Baltimore, Maryland, on one of Ravenna's old GMCs. The trailer is a 1970s vintage Troyler.

In addition to Ford cars, the Motor Convoy also delivered new Ford medium- and heavy-duty trucks. This Ford CL-9000 COE and Cottrell truck trailer is loaded with Brazilian-built Ford Cargos.

Long ago, Sober was one of the largest auto transporters in the United States. After being sold several times, Sober ended up as HSI., a division of Coltrans. When this photo was taken in 1987, HSI. had only few contracts, hauling imported vehicles. This load of Mitsubishis, seen leaving Baltimore, Maryland, is riding on a 48-foot Stuart trailer, pulled by an International 4300.

Dixie Auto Transport was another old company owned by Coltrans. Like HSI., Dixie was unable to secure a contract with a domestic auto manufacturer in the 1980s. Consequently, they were both left to transport imports, usually at a cheaper rate than the domestics paid. Ten Yugos easily fit on this International 4300 and Escott trailer.

Leaseway Motorcar Transport also hauled out of the CSX railhead in Twin Oaks, Pennsylvania, near Chester. The traffic out of Twin Oaks was primarily GM, but this load of 1987 Jeeps originated there also. The tractor is unusual in that it's a GMC Brigadier fitted with a Chevrolet Bruin grille.

Delavan embarked on an extensive rebuild program of Ryder's equipment in the mid-1980s. The most successful project was converting hundreds of old Bankhead B-6 and Delavan 2600 trailers into quick loaders, as shown here. In addition to lengthening the trailers to 48 feet, they had all-new upper decks. In 1987, Delavan offered these trailers to carriers other than Ryder. They are still popular with independents and used car dealers. *Delavan Welding*

With longer length laws in effect, the old 43-foot van trailers were stretched to 53 feet. These had been produced in limited numbers, and each Ryder company had a few. The lengthened units gained room for one more full-size van. *Delavan Welding*

The popular Delavan 2600 was also stretched to 48 feet. This stretched 2600 and Brigadier tractor is transporting nine Suzuki Samurais, forerunner of the Suzuki Sidekick and Geo Tracker. The Samurai sold well until it earned a reputation for unstable handling.

Cottrell's rebuild program also involved the old Bankhead B-series trailers. Along with a complete rebuild, the rear one-third of the trailer was redesigned, and they were lengthened to 48 feet. Nu Car had hundreds of these rebuilds in service, and they were very versatile. This one, leaving Dundalk Marine Terminal, Baltimore, Maryland, is loaded with Toyotas. Nu Car's tractor is a 1984 Ford LN-9000 with Budd wheels.

One of the rarest class-eight trucks built in modern times was the Dodge 9500 Big Horn. Fewer than 300 were built and very few saw car carrier service. Flynn Motors ran this one for a while in the 1980s. The Big Horn is highly sought after by truck collectors today.

Reliable Carriers' enclosed transporters can be seen in almost every part of the United States, delivering exotic cars. However, Reliable did operate some open transporters, and still does. This Ford LN-9000 and Bankhead trailer was caught in 1987 with a load of collectable cars. Above the cab is a 1970 Plymouth Barracuda, while on the trailer is a 1955 Chevrolet, a Chevrolet van, and a 1971 Barracuda.

The International Fleetstar A was produced from 1967 until it was replaced with the S-series in 1977. Many carriers used them, and quite a few ended up working for KAT. This one was still at work in 1986, hauling Mitsubishis out of Baltimore, Maryland. By this time, Mitsubishi was offering a complete line of autos, pickups, and an SUV, the Montero. KAT's trailer is a 48-foot Stuart.

The American Motors Corporation plant in Kenosha, Wisconsin, was one of the oldest in the country. Automobile bodies were built in one area, trucked to another plant for painting, and then returned to the main plant for final assembly. In 1987, the plant was assembling Chrysler full-size cars, along with Renault Alliance and Encore models. These Chrysler bodies are returning for final assembly on a special trailer pulled by an old International Transtar COE.

AMC also maintained a fleet of quick load auto transporters at Kenosha to move completed autos off the property. This load of Renaults is destined for an outbound rail yard in nearby Bain, Wisconsin. The tractor pulling the Stuart quick loader is an International Fleetstar A.

When there were no more Dodge heavy trucks available, Cassens switched to GMC. These 1983 Brigadiers are equipped with Stuart 10-car trailers and head racks. Except for the Mexican-built Ramcharger, this load of Chrysler vehicles originated in St. Louis, Missouri.

After buying GMCs for 10 years, Cassens switched to International in 1986. This S-2200 and Bankhead trailer is loaded with St. Louis vehicles destined for western Pennsylvania. Cassens continues to operate Internationals today.

With a base price of just under $4,000, the Yugo took the minicar market by storm. Unfortunately, poor reliability and political problems in Yugoslavia made Yugo's popularity short-lived. The Yugos that came through the Port of Baltimore were shipped inland by KAT. This load of 10 on a Mack R-model and 48-foot Bankhead trailer was at rest on the Pennsylvania Turnpike in 1987.

The Cadillac Allante was shipped in enclosed trailers during its short production run. Ryder revived the Boutell name for this project and this GMC Astro Aero, seen near Denver, Colorado, is operated by Boutell. *Mark Waterman*

In the late 1980s, Porsche began shipping its cars in enclosed equipment. Commercial Carriers and Motor Convoy were Porsche's principal carriers. Motor Convoy's Cottrell-built equipment even included an enclosed pod, hinged on the right side, above the car that accommodated one car. This rig used an International tractor, although Freightliners were also seen.

Approaching its 20th birthday, this Delavan trailer is still at work, transporting thrill show vehicles in the late 1980s. The tractor is also an oldie, a 1974 Dodge CNT-900.

Based in Utah, Neil's Transport hauled imports and used cars. This International S-2200 and Delavan 10-car rig is loaded with pizza cars.

KAT's equipment was just as varied in the 1980s as it had been in years past. This Volvo, working out of Baltimore, is seen here with a load of Suzukis. Since Volvo took over GM's heavy truck division, Volvo has become one of the most popular auto transport trucks. However, Volvos were rarely seen hauling cars in 1987, when this shot was taken.

Alfa Romeo autos are no longer imported into the United States. However, in the late 1980s, they offered a line of sedans, in addition to the sports cars that they had been famous for. This load of Alfas is being transported by Lindamood Enterprises on a custom-built Kenworth and Stuart trailer.

Robin Transport was a carrier for Volvo, Land Rover, and other high-end imports. For a while, in the 1980s, Robin was owned by TNT. This enclosed trailer, pulled by a Freightliner COE, is exiting the Dundalk Marine Terminal with a load of Volvos.

Canadian Auto Carriers (CAC) was once the largest auto transporter in western Canada. In the 1980s, it was taken over by Auto Haulaway. This Mack R-model was formerly a CAC rig, now leased to Auto Haulaway. It's loaded with GM, Ford, and Chrysler vehicles. *Bruce Brunner*

In the mid-1980s, Cottrell introduced an 11-car stinger that became one of the most popular auto transport rigs ever built. This one, an ex-Cassens rig, was still working in 1994.

For hauling bulky vehicles, like these Chevrolet Suburbans, Cottrell built this low side trailer with a three-car head rack. Most were sold to Leaseway for use by Anchor Motor Freight.

An improved model of the 11-car Cottrell was introduced about 1987. This was the CS-12, a 12-car rig. This one, operated by Nu Car Carriers, is transporting 11 Ford Escorts. The Ford LNT-9000 rig is one of the carriers that Nu Car had on order when it was bought by Leaseway. It would be one of Nu Car's last new rigs.

Bankhead produced a 12-car stinger that was almost identical to the Cottrell unit. This one, with an International S-series chassis, has been test loaded with 12 Dodge Daytonas for Cassens.

This old ex-Anchor GMC Astro car hauler has been converted to transport large trucks. In this photo, taken in Carlisle, Pennsylvania, it is hauling three large U.S. mail vans. The return trip to Ohio or Michigan will carry four Chevrolet or GMC minivans out of Baltimore, Maryland.

This GMC Astro 95 and Stuart trailer is operated by GM Engineering. Shot in Albuquerque, New Mexico, it's loaded with 1989 Chevrolet S-10 vehicles, probably show or test units. *Paul McLaughlin*

McCallum Transport was another Canadian transporter taken over by Auto Haulaway. This long-nose Ford LT-9000 had been a McCallum rig before the takeover. Note the Ford Aerostar van above the cab. The height is probably in excess of the U.S. limit of 13 feet, 6 inches. However, it's still legal in Canada at 14 feet, 2 inches or less. *Allen Neamtz*

Although Jack Cooper Transports took over United Transports in the early 1980s, most of the old United equipment continued to operate in the United's yellow color scheme. Once primarily contracted to GM, Jack Cooper began hauling Chrysler vehicles in the mid-1980s. This GMC 9500, loaded with Chrysler units, was 15 years old when this photo was taken in 1989. *Paul McLaughlin*

Jack Cooper also acquired PMT, the trucking division of the Union Pacific Railroad, in the late 1980s. However, the PMT logo and blue-and-white paint scheme is still used on equipment operated in the West. Loaded with Hondas, this Chevrolet Titan 90 is leaving the Port of Long Beach in California. This old (1970–1971) rig was doing local deliveries in 1989, but it was once a line haul rig, delivering GM autos from plants in California to several Southwestern states.

Port Terminal Transport also worked out of Long Beach, delivering Toyotas and other imports. A division of Convoy, much of its equipment was ex-Convoy or leased. This ex-Convoy GM COE could be either a GMC or Chevrolet. It's one of the units on which Convoy had removed the nameplates. Note the single-tired quick load trailer.

This GMC General is another rig leased to Port Terminal Transport. It too, is loaded with 1989 Toyotas, imported through Long Beach.

Delavan introduced a 12-car stinger in 1988, and the first ones went to the various Ryder companies. By this time, the GMC nameplate on the Brigadier was replaced with the WHITEGMC nameplate. The big Volkswagen van on the rear of the trailer limits this load to 11 units.

Leaseway's last Brigadiers were also WHITEGMC models, but with the high hood. This one is equipped with a Cottrell CS-14 14-car stinger. These 75-foot combinations used a 5-car head rack.

Just before the decade ended, WHITEGMC replaced the Brigadier with the WG. The two trucks are seen here side by side. The WG pictured is one with a cut-down cab. *James Rowe*

With their Brigadiers and WGs doing the line haul work, Ryder delegated the local deliveries and shuttle work to the old GMC 9500s. These loads of unfinished Dodge Dakotas are ready to leave Chrysler's "Dodge City" assembly plant in Warren, Michigan. They are probably destined for a containment area, where they will be held until the missing components are available. *Don Bunn*

Insured Transporters hauled a variety of imports in the Southwest. This Detroit Diesel-powered Freightliner was over 10 years old when this photo was taken in 1989. It is leaving the Port of Long Beach, California with a load of Isuzu vehicles.

For a period in the early 1980s, Freightliner did not produce its low-profile COE. The biggest purchaser of the low-profile units, Convoy, turned to Peterbilt and Kenworth for similar trucks. The Peterbilt model was called the 310 and was originally designed for use as a garbage truck. *James Rowe*

Kenworth introduced a low-cab PD-model, also intended for refuse work, in 1972. At Convoy's request, Kenworth adapted the low-cab for car-hauling applications. This one, now in Ryder yellow and lettered for Commercial Carriers, was formerly a Convoy rig. *John Heistand*

In the mid-1980s, Freightliner reintroduced an improved low-profile cab model that was ideal for high-capacity auto transport equipment. Operated by Jack Cooper Transports, this Freightliner is loaded with 1989 GM autos that were built in Arlington, Texas. Note that the Freightliner nameplates have been removed or covered up by Jack Cooper's own logo. This was probably done to prevent offending GM, which was Jack Cooper's principal shipper. *John Heistand*

Sometimes, one carrier's surplus equipment ends up in a competitor's fleet. Now leased to CTC, this Ford W-series previously served Hadley, in California. *Mark Waterman*

Loaded with 10 1989 Camaros and Firebirds, this Brigadier is operated by Janesville Auto Transport. Except for the company lettering on the door, all of Ryder's U.S. carriers were painted and lettered the same.

After the Canadian carriers MCL and ACL became part of Ryder, their equipment started to appear in Ryder's yellow paint scheme. When new equipment, such as this WHITEGMC Brigadier, was added to the Canadian fleet, Ryder used equipment that was almost identical to its U.S. rigs. The amber fog lights are the only visible difference between this MCL 12-car rig and its U.S. brothers. *Allen Neamtz*

The 1990s

The Present and the Future

By the 1990s, the auto transport industry had developed into two distinct groups; the large union (mostly Teamster) carriers serving the auto makers, and the independent carriers serving the auctions and used car dealers. There was some overlap in both areas with the new car carriers hauling lease cars and a few independents hauling new imported autos. Mergers and buyouts continued and many long-established names in the industry disappeared.

Until the mid-1990s, most of the companies that Ryder had acquired continued to operate under the former names. In 1995, the decision was made to consolidate all the automobile transporters under one name. The name chosen was Commercial Carriers, Ryder's largest auto hauler and a name known nationwide. Ryder had owned Boutell since the early 1980s, but most of the Boutell terminals and operations were combined into other Ryder companies with similar authorities. Boutell was one of the oldest names in the

auto transport industry, but the name saw only limited use by Ryder. In 1995, Ryder revived the Boutell name and gave it to its division that delivered new medium- and heavy-duty trucks. Previously, two Ryder companies, Commercial Carriers and Fleet Carrier Corp. had done the bulk of these deliveries. The Boutell name also reappeared on a few auto transporters in the late 1990s but the M&G, Complete, JATCO, and Convoy names disappeared. In 1996, Ryder announced that its automobile carrier group, the largest in the nation, was for sale. Although very profitable in some years, pressure from the auto makers to reduce costs and increased demands from the unions reduced Ryder's profitability.

Allied expanded its operations into the Northeast, serving Ford, Chrysler, and GM at both railheads and assembly plants. By 1997, Allied had grown to become the Number Two auto carrier in the nation, behind Ryder. In May of that year, Allied Holdings (Allied's parent company) agreed to purchase Ryder for $114.5 million

In the early 1990s, Nu Car Carriers was operating as a division of Leaseway Transportation. This Ford LN-9000, with a two-car head rack and rebuilt trailer, is one of the rigs that Nu Car had owned before the takeover. Before long, Leaseway replaced Nu Car's equipment with old ex-Anchor GMCs.

Williams trailers and head racks were popular in the West. This load of Mitsubishi Montero SUVs is riding on Williams equipment operated by Dealer's Auto Transport, Inc. The tractor is a Peterbilt 352.

in cash and the assumption of certain liabilities. By October, the deal was done, and Allied became the largest auto transporter in the United States and Canada, hauling 65 percent of new vehicle shipments. The highway carrier operation was eventually renamed Allied Automotive Group (AAG), and that logo now appears on the old Allied equipment along with the ex-Ryder rigs.

KAT continued limited operations in the 1990s, hauling mostly Toyota vehicles and various medium-duty domestic and Japanese trucks. Later, the truck-hauling operation was renamed Auto Truck Transport. In the mid-1990s, the KAT name also disappeared. Automotive Carrier Services (ACS) and Active Transportation purchased KAT's parent company, Jupiter Transportation. These companies were Kentucky-based vehicle carriers, established about 1987 and contracting initially with Ford Motor Company. Their highway carriers were ACS, Safety Carriers, and Active Transportation. In 1994, after acquiring and operating KAT and Auto Truck for a short time, they incorporated both companies into Active and ACS. Active and Safety also received contracts from importers in the South and East. ACS also has a division called Unimark, which serves the large rental companies and the auto auction industry.

Throughout the late 1980s, Leaseway Transportation had been looking for a buyer for the part of its

The Ford F-series pickup became America's best-selling vehicle in the 1990s. They were built at several locations in the United States and Canada. These 1991 Fords are being shuttled from an assembly plant in Canada to the CSX railhead in New Boston, Michigan. Auto Haulaway is the carrier, and the tractor is a GMC Brigadier.

Also bound for New Boston is this load of full-size 1991 Fords and Mercurys on a new WHITEGMC COE. These Auto Haulaway tractors are driven by owner-operators.

auto-transporting business that delivered autos other than those produced by GM. After several unsuccessful offers, it sold the entire auto transport operation to the Penske organization. When the sale was completed, the Nu Car and Anchor names disappeared and Penske retained only the Leaseway logo on the trucks. Although Leaseway does transport a few other autos, it is again largely a GM carrier in the East.

The number of independent transporters grew in the 1990s, and many of their fleets grew in size until they rivaled some of the union carriers. In 1998, a company was formed called United Road Services (URS) with the intention of forming the nation's first national nonunion auto hauling and towing network. Originally, seven companies were purchased, with five more added in 1999. So far, most of URS' business involves hauling used and off-lease vehicles, and it remains to be

Peterbilts in Ryder colors were rare. This one, owned by Freddie Nelson, was leased to Commercial Carriers. The trailer is a Delavan 2600 that has been stretched to 48-feet. Freddie's load is 10 Mazdas. *Freddie Nelson*

This may be the World's largest Peterbilt auto transport tractor. This four-axle, quadruple bunk rig was the flagship of Flynn Motors' fleet. The 48-foot Bankhead trailer is loaded with classic cars.

192

seen if it or other independents can obtain contracts from the major auto makers.

In the 1980s, minivans, pickups, and sport utility vehicles (SUVs) increased in sales, while automobile production fell. The Ford F-150 became the best-selling vehicle in America. This trend continued into the 1990s, with almost every auto maker offering a minivan or SUV. In the 1980s, the auto transporters were buying equipment that could haul as many automobiles as possible. However, the bulk and weight of these larger vehicles meant that usually only 8 or 9 could be transported

on equipment designed for 12 or 13 autos. Trailer manufacturers began to offer equipment that better suited the loads of larger vehicles. This equipment usually had fewer individual decks, stronger hydraulics, and low-profile cabs. Allied purchased some low-profile Freightliner COEs with special Bankhead trailers for transporting Ford Explorers. These lightweight units could legally transport 10 Explorers. With the federal gross weight limit at 80,000 pounds, 10 SUVs on lightweight equipment appears to be the maximum legal load. The auto transporters and the NATA have tried unsuccessfully to

These 1991 Chevrolet S-10s have just crossed the Ambassador Bridge into Canada from Detroit. Leaseway Motorcar Transport will take them to a Canadian carrier's loading yard where they will be reloaded for delivery in Canada or the Northeastern United States. This quick load trailer with single tires is pulled by a hybrid GMC/Chevrolet tractor.

Its rare to see an R-model Mack hauling cars, especially in Ryder's colors. This R-model, owned by David Frost, hauled Toyotas and other imports in the Chicago area. *Freddie Nelson*

The Auto Bus operates from the Northeastern states to Florida. While their customers travel south by other means, their autos are shipped on open carriers like this Freightliner. Note the two-car head rack. *Harry Patterson*

Strictly by coincidence, this RCMP Chevrolet and Auto Haulaway Kenworth are painted in matching colors. This photo was taken before Auto Haulaway's takeover by Allied Holdings. Today, the rig would be white and green. *Bruce Brunner*

Toyota has a large processing center near Baltimore, Maryland, and several carriers haul out of it. DMT Trucking is the operator of this International S-2200 and 48-foot Cottrell trailer. The driver needs only to lower the 4-Runner riding above the cab before starting out for his destination. In its present position, it is overheight.

Before going bankrupt, Coltrans eliminated the Dixie and HSI names from its rigs and ran under the Coltrans logo. This International is a leased unit hauling Mazdas out of the railhead in Chicago. *Freddie Nelson*

The bow tie on the hood of this ACL rig identifies it as a Chevrolet Bruin. However, the grille has been replaced with one from its GMC cousin, the Brigadier. Next to the bow tie is a small Ryder logo indicating that this photo was taken after Ryder's takeover of ACL. *Owen Barcomb*

Hot Shots are medium-duty tractors combined with long flat trailers that specialize in hauling loads that are bulky but lightweight. Hot Shot Express was the carrier of these front-wheel drive mail vans when this photo was taken in 1990.

Some carriers still relied on military vehicles for a source of revenue in the 1990s. This load of M151A2s is loaded on a Lindamood Enterprises Kenworth and Stuart high side trailer. *Mark Waterman*

When Ryder's old Delavan 2300 trailers began to wear out, they were scrapped. However, many of the Brigadier tractors were still usable. They combined the tractors with the old 48-foot quick loader trailers and made up rigs like this. The trailer's gooseneck and kingpin had to be reworked to match up with the stinger's fifth wheel. Most of these rigs saw service in Florida. *Owen Barcomb*

get federal weight limits for auto transports raised to 97,000 pounds, possibly by distributing the weight over six axles instead of five. However, it remains at 80,000 pounds everywhere except in a few western states.

In 1997, Freightliner took over Ford's heavy-duty truck building operations and renamed the trucks Sterling. Model for model, the Sterlings retained the Ford styling and the L-model remained the equivalent of the old Louisville. A special Car Hauler model, the L9500, was introduced in 1999. On this vehicle, the cab is mounted 4 inches lower on the special chassis and the suspension modifications include a 5-inch dropped axle. This effectively reduces the overall height and makes the tractor competitive with Volvo and International's special models.

In the past, many of the smaller independent companies used secondhand equipment, much of it castoff by the larger carriers. Throughout the 1980s, some of the independents began buying premium tractors and late model stinger equipment. The Peterbilt has become quite popular with them, and Cottrell now offers car-hauling equipment specifically designed for owner-operators and independents who own Peterbilts, Kenworths, and other premium tractors. Although any make of trailer can be seen in use, the Cottrells and Boydstuns seem to be favorites of the owner-operators.

The use of enclosed trailers expanded in the 1990s. In addition to the curtain side rigs developed in the 1980s, the use of conventional appearing van trailers grew. Chrysler's Dodge Viper and Plymouth Prowler are delivered in enclosed trailers operated by Reliable Moving and Storage. Although especially built to transport autos, the trailers look similar to conventional moving vans. J. B. Hunt and Swift Transportation also transport new vehicles in hard side trailers. Allied, Leaseway, and other carriers have enclosed trailers, which are used for

Centurion Auto Transport was a big carrier of import cars in the South. This GMC Brigadier and Cottrell trailer is transporting three Chevrolet Suburbans destined for export to a Middle East country.

transporting high-dollar imports, in their fleets. However, it's possible to see the rigs unloading common family sedans, which are sometimes hauled as back hauls.

The railroads continue to handle most of the long-distance shipment of new vehicles and even a few used cars, when they are shipped bulk into locations with rail facilities nearby. The importers made greater use of the railroads in the 1990s, partly because they are now building autos in U.S. assembly plants. Some of these assembly plants are joint ventures with U.S. auto makers and the importers began using the same distribution channels as their U.S. partners. European imports are able to make greater use of East Coast ports, as the railroads have established a "land bridge" to ship their autos west. This is a dedicated express service that saves the importers many days time over transporting the units by ship through the Panama Canal.

As the 1990s come to a close, only the F. J. Boutell name remains of the original 16 NATA members. However, a few other long-established companies are still hauling cars. Among them are Cassens, E&L, Hadley, Jack Cooper Transports, Mack's Transport Service, and PMT.

The Ford Explorer became one of the best-selling SUVs in the 1990s. This load of 1991 Fords was transported by Nu Car Carriers on an ex-Anchor Chevrolet Bruin. The tractor is one that Leaseway had lengthened and converted from a high fifth wheel to stinger. The trailer is a Cottrell CS-10; a quick load model built in the late 1980s. After Leaseway disposed of Nu Car's Fords, these CS-10s were Nu Car's standard transport rig.

This rear view of the Centurion rig shows the details of the Suburban, which appears to be an ambulance conversion. Note the Red Crescent, the Arabic equivalent of the Red Cross.

One of the most unusual auto transporters has to be this American LaFrance rig, based on an old fire truck chassis. Up to four cars could be transported on the truck's two decks and another was towed behind on a two-wheel dolly.

Sometimes, the unusual vehicle is not the transporter but the vehicles transported. The auto on the rear of this Reliable Carriers open trailer is a prototype Cadillac. Its styling features have been disguised with black tape in the wheel opening area and red tape around the taillights. *Elliott Kahn*

These 15-year-old Dodges were still in use in 1990. Originally West Coast rigs with Williams head racks, they finished their careers with Ryder in Florida. *Elliott Kahn*

Hadley served the railhead in Denver, where this load of Fords was shot in 1990. The Ford LN-9000 tractor has a Williams head rack and trailer. Note the four-door dually pickup on the top deck.

This 12-car Cottrell is being fully utilized with this load of imported Chevrolet Geo models. Note how closely the units are loaded to each other. *Paul McLaughlin*

The cab on this F-series Ford is lower than that of its bigger brother, the Louisville. The few inches of extra clearance allow this big Dodge van to ride above the cab legally. These 1991 Dodge B-series vans were built in Windsor, Canada.

Nine Toyotas can be seen here on a Ford LN-9000 and 48-foot Bankhead trailer operated by KAT. Note the small tires on the tractor's tag or pusher axle.

By 1992, KAT's fleet of 48-foot Bankheads was beginning to be replaced by these International 8200 stingers. These rigs were leased to KAT by ACS and soon ACS would take over KAT's car-hauling operations.

Most of the Chevrolet Corvette production moves out by truckaway. In 1992, Leaseway was the carrier for areas in the Northeast. Leaseway's tractor is a WHITEGMC WG with a cut-down cab.

The HMMWV or Hummer, replaced the Jeep in the U.S. military. This load of five military Hummers is transported on a Delavan van trailer. The tractor is a Freightliner.

The lack of vehicles to transport hasn't stopped this owner-operator. He's turned to hauling livestock, maybe until the auto business picks up again. This tractor is also a Freightliner.

The independent transporters are likely to be seen operating any kind of tractor. Petra Transportation operated this Kenworth COE and long quick load trailer in Oklahoma.

The Superliner was Mack's premium long-nose tractor in the 1980s. This Canadian Superliner, with its winter front in place, is leased to Auto Haulaway and is hauling 1990 Fords. *Bruce Brunner*

By the early 1990s, most of Ryder's company-owned equipment was stinger-steered and brokers used the old high fifth wheel trailers. This Brigadier and 48-foot quick loader is loaded with Jeep Wranglers. Note the small grille, slope hood Brigadier in the background.

DMT Trucking put some of these Cottrell 10-car stingers in its fleet in the late 1980s. This one is based on an International S-2200 Auto Hauler chassis. When retired by the big fleets, these high side Cottrells are sought after by the independent carriers.

Auto Elite Transport was a new company started up in the 1990s, after Nu Car's demise. Many of its drivers and much of its equipment was ex-Nu Car. This load of seven Range Rovers is leaving the Dundalk Marine Terminal in Baltimore.

Auto Convoy operated a few of these Escott stingers with International S-series tractors for a few years in the 1980s. The unusual rigs then went to Coltrans, where they also had a short career. In the 1990s, most were sold to independents and owner-operators. This one, still in Auto Convoy's blue and white, is on its third career, hauling used cars in Florida. *Russell MacNeil*

This Peterbilt 352 has an interesting heritage. Originally a Convoy tractor, it would have been painted yellow and lettered "Commercial Carriers" after the Ryder takeover. Now, with Allied's logo on the doors, it's still at work, delivering imports out of the California ports. The trailer is a late model Delavan fast load. *Mark Wayman*

In addition to its fleet of enclosed transporters, Robin Transport also operated some open carriers. This late 1970s Ford LN-9000 and Stuart trailer is ex-Hadley Auto Transport.

The Chevrolet Kodiak and GMC Top Kick were GM's medium-duty trucks in the 1980s. This Kodiak is pretty husky, with tandem axles and a small sleeper. The W&K trailer is loaded with thrill show vehicles, which are also Chevrolets. *Mark Waterman*

Reliable Carriers is the transporter for Chrysler's sports cars, the Dodge Viper and Plymouth Prowler. The two-deck enclosed trailers are pulled by long-nose premium tractors, usually fitted with big sleepers. This tractor is a Peterbilt.

The Ford Probe was built in the Ford and Mazda plant in Flat Rock, Michigan. This load of nine Probes is transported by Allied Systems on an old (1981) International S-2200 and Bankhead stinger. Although once a line haul truck, by the mid-1990s, it was used for local deliveries.

After Ryder's takeover of Convoy, most of Convoy's equipment was transferred to Commercial Carriers. This Freightliner day cab with Westland trailer and head rack is now hauling Mazdas out of California for Commercial.

These 1992 Fords are about to be unloaded from an Allied System's rig in Des Moines, Iowa. The Ford L-9000 and Cottrell trailer had formerly been lettered for Auto Convoy. *Paul McLaughlin*

The trucks in the ACS fleets, Active Transportation and Safety Carrier, Inc., are painted in Safety Yellow, as used on emergency vehicles. This International 8200 and Cottrell trailer is loaded with Infiniti luxury autos.

This sleeper-equipped Ford is unloading in Vanderhoof, British Columbia. The panels leaning against the side of the trailer protect the bottom cars from flying gravel in transit.

The Kenworth T-800 is more often seen doing construction work than hauling cars. However, Waggoner's Trucking operated several, beginning in the late 1980s. This one, with a Williams head rack and trailer, is loaded with off-lease Jeep Cherokees. *Mark Waterman*

Allied Van Lines was the operator of this Kenworth T-600B and rebuilt Bankhead trailer. These van lines rigs were often seen only partially loaded. *Harry Patterson*

Flynn Motors' black rigs are a common sight on the East Coast. Most of its fleet is based on Peterbilt conventional tractors, but a few other makes, like this International Eagle, are also used. *Harry Patterson*

Modern transport equipment loads the top decks first. The decks are then raised and the bottom units are loaded. Unloading is done in reverse. This Peterbilt conventional with a setback axle is operated by Sierra Mountain Express. The Williams trailer has its top deck loaded. *Mark Waterman*

The 8200 is the International that is used in the auto transport industry today. Its short hood and low cab are ideally suited for auto transport applications. This 8200, with a low side Cottrell trailer, is operated by MPG Transport, transporting Volvos.

In the northeastern United States, Subarus are distributed by several different distributors. This Brigadier and Cottrell trailer was leased to the Subaru Distributor Corp. in Orangeburg, New York. Normally, it would be seen loaded with Subarus, but this shot shows a back haul of used cars. *Allen Neamtz*

In the early 1990s, Leaseway Transportation reconditioned some of its Brigadiers and had these 75-foot Bankhead outfits built up on them. This eight-car load of Astro vans shows how versatile the rigs were.

This view shows how the Astro vans were positioned on the head rack. Five small cars could be loaded in this same space.

Complete Auto Transit, Inc., operated several hundred of the Delavan 2800-series stingers. The driver of this Brigadier, photographed near Carlisle, Pennsylvania, in 1993, has already delivered 3 of the 10 Corvettes that were in this load. Since each dealer usually receives only one Corvette at a time, he probably has seven more stops to make.

This big Peterbilt with a big walk-in sleeper is just the rig to deliver this big cargo, Lincoln stretch limousines.
Harry Patterson

The big Peterbilts are favorites of owner-operators and independent used car haulers. Note the three-axle Cottrell trailer behind this "Pete." Like the trailers of the 1930s, this one is equipped with single tires. *Harry Patterson*

Allied Systems rebuilt much of its equipment in the 1980s and much of that equipment is still in service. This Bankhead quick loader was built on an early 1980s Ford LN-9000 tractor. The wheelbase has been stretched to accommodate the five-car head rack. The autos are Korean-built Ford Aspires. *Russell MacNeil*

The Dodge Ram pickup was completely restyled for 1994. The "big truck" styling caused Dodges sales to skyrocket and forced Ford and GM to rethink the light-duty truck styling. This Cassens' International 8200 is loaded with Dodge Rams and Dakotas. *Dave Faust*

Leased to Auto Haulaway, this GMC 5-Star General is unloading in British Columbia. The Ford Windstar above the cab is ready to come off next. Note the curtain protecting the units in the belly of the trailer from gravel and stones. *Bruce Brunner*

This Ryder WG, loaded with Fords, is also fitted with protection curtains. These rigs are operating in the state of Washington, hauling out of a railhead. Note this low-cab WG is able to transport the F-series pickup level, above the cab. *Dave Faust*

This is another rebuilt Allied Ford, but with a four-car head rack and Bankhead low side trailer. These Ford F-series pickups were built in Norfolk, Virginia.

This view shows how tightly this load of F-series pickups have been loaded. Note the truck above the cab and how its rear wheels have been lowered on the Number Two deck until they are almost in the bed of the truck below.

Like Cottrell and Bankhead, Delavan also introduced a low side, quick load trailer. The earliest examples were mounted on reconditioned Brigadier chassis. This one is hauling Chrysler LH cars, built in the ex-AMC plant in Bramlea, Ontario. Note the small tires on the pusher axle.

Ryder received contracts to haul Ford products in the early 1990s. As a result, and for the first time, some company-owned Fords were added to its fleet. This L-9000 has been built as a low side quick loader by Delavan. *Dave Faust*

The Boutell name was assigned to the Ryder company that specialized in the transportation of medium- and heavy-duty trucks. The tractors, like this WHITEGMC, were driven by owner-operators. This load is made up of five Chevrolet Kodiak cab and chassis units.

In the mid-1990s, Auto Haulaway, the largest auto carrier in Canada, was bought out by Allied Holdings, the parent company of Allied Systems. Working in Allied's green and white, this Auto Haulaway International is headed to Detroit with a load of 1996 Dodge vans built in Windsor, Ontario.

Also bound for Detroit is this load of Chrysler minivans on an Auto Haulaway Ford. The LN-9000 tractor and Teal trailer is still painted in Auto Haulaway's colors of blue and white.

Reliable Carriers' open carriers are just as fancy as their enclosed units. This Kenworth T-600B, fitted with a Bankhead head rack and low side trailer, is loaded with Range Rovers. *Harry Patterson*

Hadley has always operated Ford equipment in its West Coast-based fleet. In the 1990s, its new equipment included many of these Cottrell quick load stingers. This L-9000 is loaded with Korean-built Kias. *Mark Wayman*

North of the border, Ryder purchased two Canadian carriers, MCL and ACL. When new equipment was added to the Canadian fleets, it was based on the equipment that Ryder operated in the "lower 48." This WG, operated by Transport MCL Ryder, has been equipped with a handrail above the cab, required in Canada. *Francois Spenard*

The low-profile Freightliner reappeared in many auto transport fleets in the mid-1990s. This one, operated by Ryder, is outfitted with a Delavan 12-car rig. *Dave Faust*

One of the most popular trucks ever produced was the B-series Mack. This 1964 B-70-series Mack was still working in the 1990s. Note the long wheelbase required with the sleeper and Stuart three-car head rack. *Neil Sherff*

Allied's enclosed rigs that had been used exclusively for transporting Porsche cars in the 1980s were still in service in the 1990s. The Porsche logos have been removed because Allied was also transporting other high-dollar imports in enclosed rigs. Note the pod above the cab of this Freightliner and how far it extends forward. *Mark Wayman*

The WHITEGMC WG was adopted by many fleets as their standard tractor. This WG, operated by Eagle Auto Transport of Jacksonville, Florida is loaded with 11 Toyotas. Unlike the Ryder WGs with their cut-down cabs, this unit has a standard height cab. *Russell MacNeil*

Eagle also operated enclosed equipment like this WG with a sleeper box and stinger-steered trailer. Shot in Denver, Colorado, this truck was far from home. *Mark Waterman*

Based in Vancouver, Washington, CTC was a large carrier of imported autos in the Northwest. Much of its equipment was similar to that operated by the other northwestern carrier, Convoy. This 1980 Peterbilt COE was outfitted with head rack and trailer by Westland Manufacturing Company, Convoy's trailer-building subsidiary. Note the ladder, which allows the driver to reach the tie downs for the auto above the cab. *Dave Faust*

Centurion Auto Transport was another company hauling imports out of Jacksonville, Florida. Centurion got its start hauling Toyotas in the early 1970s. The two different style Freightliners seen here are among a wide variety of equipment that Centurion operates. *Russell MacNeil*

Freightliner became the best-selling heavy truck in the 1990s. United Van Lines is using this one for transporting its client's cars with an old Cottrell humped trailer. Note the GPS pod, mounted on a stalk behind the sleeper. *Harry Patterson*

In the 1990s, Leaseway Transportation was purchased by the Penske organization. With a few exceptions, it went back to being a dedicated GM carrier, serving the Eastern United States. This WG is loaded with Chevrolet Cavaliers.

Auto Truck Transport is the company that delivers many medium- and heavy-duty trucks. This Peterbilt conventional is loaded with Japanese Nissan UDs. The trailer is a Cottrell unit, especially built for hauling trucks. *Harry Patterson*

Eight-car enclosed rigs, like this Freightliner, were developed in the 1990s. This one, with an over cab sleeper, is operated by Waggoners Trucking. Allied and Leaseway operate similar rigs. *Russell MacNeil*

Allied Systems purchased a fleet of these low-profile Freightliners for transporting Ford Explorers. The compact cab allowed up to 10 Explorers to be transported within a 75-foot overall length. *Joseph Wanchura*

In 1997, Allied Holdings bought Ryder's auto carrier division. Along with the acquisition came equipment like this old Brigadier that had been reconditioned in the early 1990s. This truck must have seen some service in Canada, because it is equipped with a handrail above the cab. *Russell MacNeil*

For owner-operators who prefer premium equipment, Cottrell builds the Classic Pro 4-series trailers and head racks. They have been designed especially for use with the Peterbilt conventional tractor.

Cottrell's Classic Pro 4-series trailer and head rack was designed with owner-operators in mind. This Peterbilt is dressed to the nines, with chrome trim everywhere, including the sides of the head rack. *Harry Patterson*

This pair of Ryder WGs, operated by Complete Auto Transit, Inc., have brought these 1994 Corvettes from Kentucky to Nevada. They'll spend the night here before continuing with deliveries in the morning. *James Rowe*

Vanderhoof, British Columbia, is pretty far from Canada's metropolitan areas. The trailer on this Ford L-9000 is equipped with side panels and curtains to protect the bottom cars from road hazards on the way. *Bruce Brunner*

Modern auto transporters have grown so big and have so much capacity that weight has become a factor. With an 80,000-pound weight limit enforced in most areas, carriers must try to save weight wherever possible. Besides being built of lightweight trailer components, this low-cab WG, operated by Leaseway Transportation, is equipped with aluminum wheels.

This Metro trailer and head rack is based on the old Stuart design. Using a Freightliner tractor and Metro equipment, Reliable Carriers is hauling special edition Range Rovers and used vehicles. *Neil Sherff*

Reliable Carriers is best known for its fleet of enclosed rigs, many of which deliver Chrysler's Dodge Viper and Plymouth Prowler to dealers throughout the United States. This long-nose "Pete" has to be one of the most colorful auto transporters around. *Neil Sherff*

Better-All Auto Transport is based in Washington, but its flamed rigs can be seen as far east as Pennsylvania and New Jersey. This Ford "Aero-Max" is equipped with a Boydstun trailer and head rack. *Dave Faust*

Index